THE KILLING FIELDS OF CAMBODIA

SURVIVING A LIVING HELL

SOKPHAL DIN

ap

ISBN 9789493056749 (ebook)

ISBN 9789493056732 (paperback)

Publisher: Amsterdam Publishers, The Netherlands

Editor: Suzy Thurley

info@amsterdampublishers.com

Copyright © Sokphal Din, 2020

All Rights Reserved. No part of this publication may be reproduced or transmitted in any form or by any means, electronic or mechanical, including photocopy, recording or any other information storage and retrieval system.

In memory of my late mother

Mrs Pan Penh You (Naret)

PREFACE

This book is dedicated to my mother, to my relatives and friends who lost their lives in the Killing Fields from 1975 to 1979. At the time mother began to keep a diary, documenting what our family endured in those years. Afterwards, she kept saying to me that I should write our story so that it would never be forgotten. Others told me that it was all in the past, that it was best to move on and forget about it. My perspective on this, however, is clear. It is up to me to honour my mother's wishes by telling the world of our harrowing survival. This is the only legacy that I have.

We should never forget. I lost my brother, father, grandmother and various other members of my family due to executions, starvation, disease and being worked to death in labour camps. After we were forced out of our home in Phnom Penh in 1975, within just two months, my father, four uncles and two of my teenage cousins were taken away by the Khmer Rouge. None of them ever returned.

Some three weeks before my mother's death in 2001, I was leaving her house to spend a weekend away with friends. She stood at the back door as I put on my shoes and said to me, "You are my best son. You have been good to me. You have looked after me, your sister and brother. You have provided a house for us to live in, you've never been in debt. You are the best son."

Although I was pleased to hear her words, I also felt embarrassed. And so, I simply listened and continued to put on my shoes in silence.

When she passed away on the 19th of October 2001, I realised that those words were her gift to me. Her diary revealed further gifts and dreams for the family that had been destroyed by the Khmer Rouge regime.

What I will describe in this memoir happened a long time ago in a far-away country, but my memories, like my feelings, have stayed sharp.

I still dream about my family, the jungle, the Killing Fields in Khmer, and the language of my youth. I tried to write about it in English but sometimes my words falter and fail me.

My mother's memory has inspired me to write. Now that I have done so, I hope that she would be proud of me.

Sokphal Din BEM

INTRODUCTION

The Cambodian Civil War was a bloody and intricate affair. Influences from both sides were numerous and far reached. On one side were the government forces and the Khmer Republic who were supported by American aerial bombings and financial aid, and South Vietnam's ground troops. On the other side, the Khmer Rouge were supported by North Vietnam, the Viet Cong, and foreign aid from Mao Zedong's Communist Party of China.

After years of violent combat, it was the Khmer Rouge who emerged victorious, with Pol Pot as their leader. A combination of Marxist, Maoist, xenophobic, and nationalist elements, the Khmer Rouge's ideology came to fruition. They rounded up city dwellers, so-called 'new' people, and placed us into rural, communal living spaces, or labour camps. We were a symbol of the old regime and were only good to be put to work, re-educated, or eliminated. The rural communities, or 'base' people, were romanticised and it was thought that through sheer human will power and agricultural autarky, Cambodia would become a functioning Communist society.

They installed their ideology through mass extermination, torture, fear, starvation, and monstrous acts. The Killing Fields, now preserved as a memorial site, consist of 127 mass graves containing

20,000 bodies. For me, it was a place where we worked tirelessly in inhumane conditions. It was estimated that between 1.7 and 2.5 million people were killed – a quarter of Cambodia's population.

Mass graves (Photo credit DC-CAM)

"No profit to keep you. No loss to extract you" were the painful words that the Khmer Rouge used to insult us. Their words were engraved deep into our memories, we had no value as human beings, we received no compassion or care, and we were in the grasps of their extreme and inhumane power.

* * *

1979. They took me to an abandoned barn. My arms, my wrists were tied behind my back. Hay was scattered in the middle of the barn, and wooden blocks were dispersed on the ground. There were two of them. One was a soldier dressed in full uniform and carrying a pistol on his waist. They ordered me to kneel on the ground.

The questions began.

They asked me about my name and family background. Whatever I answered, they never seemed satisfied. The soldier kicked me each time I delivered an answer that was not to his liking. They took me by the arms and placed me on a wooden block under a beam in the middle of the barn. My wrists were tightly bound behind my back. The soldier tossed the end of the rope up and over the beam and tied it to a pillar. Then he kicked the wooden block away. The pain ripped through me – an excruciating, screaming, unbearable pain. My wrists were burning with fire since the whole weight of my body was on them. I could hear my own screams while nearly passing out.

This is what it had come to.

After everything I had been through, it would end here. Memories and images flashed through the pain. Forced from my house at gunpoint by the Khmer Rouge, we were marched into the jungle and left to die, starved, and worked almost to death in the Killing Fields and conscripted into the Khmer Rouge to fight against the Vietnamese.

I had survived almost four years of living hell under Pol Pot's regime only to die here. It was like living in a prison without walls.

Remains of victims (Photo credit DC-CAM)

1

Before.

I remember a cabinet that my father made before we were forced to flee from our house. It was a beautiful mahogany sideboard that he was very proud of. It consisted of two separate compartments and was used to store important documents and precious jewellery. Before we were forced out, my mother put all the photographs of our family, and everything that documented our lives inside. We would come back home in a day or two was what we were told by the Khmer Rouge soldiers. But we never returned, and it was as though my family ceased to exist.

The Killing Fields took everything. When I try to think of my family, I can only search the fragments of memories that I have.

Mother told me stories about our lives before the war. She told me about my grandfather to whom she was very close. He was well-educated and had an important job overseeing the Post Office in Phnom Penh when the French ruled Cambodia. My grandfather was also addicted to opium. Under the French colonial regime, many top officials in the Cambodian government were encouraged by the

French to take opium. It was an easy way for them to gain control of Khmer people.

His addiction drained the family of all the money that it had – he spent everything on drugs. Because times were difficult, my grandmother had to work hard to find extra income to support the family. She had to feed the children, buy clothes, pay the school fees, and buy opium for my grandfather.

Every day, my mum had to get up at 3 am or 4 am. She would help my grandmother to prepare the food that they would sell in the morning in front of the house. If there was time, mother would read her schoolbooks or recite her sums by the light of the fire.

The dish that we would cook on a regular basis was a traditional Khmer food called Nom Banh Chock, fine soft rice noodles with herbs and a fish soup served with different kinds of fresh vegetables. It is one of my favourite Khmer dishes and my mum would serve it to us on special occasions.

My grandfather was determined that his daughter should be properly schooled. Despite the lack of money, he insisted that my mother should be sent to school to receive an education that few girls in Cambodia had. Her two elder brothers were sent to school, but this was not the done thing for girls in Cambodian society. My mum remembers the arguments that her parents had about her schooling. My grandmother herself could not read or write and had doubts about girls being educated. She thought that if my mum were able to write she would pen love letters and disobey her parents. She was an old-fashioned lady, and strict in the traditional, Cambodian way. It was very fortunate that my mother was eventually allowed to attend school.

When my mum turned sixteen, according to the old Cambodian custom *Chol Ma Lub* (enter the shade), she was ordered by her parents to stay inside a dimmed room for three months. Her skin was given herbal treatments to make her beautiful and she had to eat certain foods which were said to make her pretty and improve her health.

My grandmother had taken a few of her nephews to live under her care. Their parents were poor farmers in a remote area. They were unable to find accommodation for their sons in the city, but my grandmother took them under her care. She provided them place to live, foods etc.

One of her nephews, named Gar, was secretly in loved with my mother. Gar was older than her and had a good job. He begged her not to marry my father but failed to stop her as she would never do anything to upset her parents or disobey their wishes. At the end Gar fell ill, he began coughing blood and later died. I suppose he was broken hearted. My mother never said that she loved him, but she felt terrible after his death.

Tol Phom heard about my mother. Apparently, he had found out about her from a neighbour. He sent some friends and relatives to ask my grandparents' permission to marry her, but my mum did not want to marry him at all. Personally, she felt she was too young to get married and wanted to continue her education. However, my grandfather was in poor health and he had told her that he would like to see her wedding before he died. So, my mum was caught between having the future she envisaged and obeying her father's wishes.

After much consideration, she felt that it was her duty to respect my grandfather and do as he had asked. My grandmother was very pleased because my father promised to build a large Khmer-style family house, wooden, pillared, and with three roof tiles, in time for the wedding.

After they got married, my mother moved in with her new husband in their newly built home where she became a housewife and helped with her husband's business. At first, my father was a kind and loving husband.

A few years later, my grandfather died. My mum was closer to her father than she was to her mother because he was educated and therefore was able to better understand her. She was very upset by his death.

My parents made a living as entrepreneurs. They had a shop in Phnom Penh behind the Royal Palace and another workshop in the Toul Svay Prey area, where they produced goods to sell in the shop. They sold religious statues of Buddha made from cement, framed pictures of Buddha painted on glass, and canvas Buddha story pictures that were needed for funeral ceremonies, tombs, and temples.

The business did not make my parents rich, but it did well enough to employ a fair number of workers. Days in the shop, I think, were good ones for my mother.

One day, she had a miscarriage and my parents prayed that she would get pregnant again. Much to her surprise, one day, a neighbour paid her a visit and told my mum that she had seen a light in the sky that resembled a shooting star. The neighbour believed that it was a divinity that had dropped on the roof of our house, which she interpreted as a good sign. She assured my mum that she would get pregnant soon, which indeed was the case.

The monsoon came the night I was born. It had heavily rained all day and into the night, so much so that the roads were flooded in many parts of Phnom Penh city. My father took my mother to the hospital in the car which unfortunately broke down on the way because of the flooding. He was very panicked and stood in the rain completely soaked; it must have been quite a scene.

My mother had difficulty giving birth. She told me this story many times over as she wanted to remind me that my father loved me very much, not caring that he was soaking wet and cold in the rain. I was born, and he adored his first son.

A short time after my birth, my father began to treat my mother badly. Later, she came to understand his uncharacteristic change in behaviour. It turned out that he was in serious debt because he had borrowed money to build the house as a wedding gift, causing a lot of arguments. I was told that my father had not been faithful to her. During this time, my mother was made to suffer physical as well as emotional torment.

Looking back, I think that my father must have loved my mum, but he was much older, and their age difference must have made him jealous. My mum retained her beauty, which fuelled his jealousy and anger.

My dad wasted all their hard-earned money on gambling and getting drunk almost every single evening. He called our neighbours to join him and play cards or *Ah porng* អាប៉ោង, a kind of gambling game, made from a small ivory spinning top. It was a six-sided die with a pin in the centre, like a dreidel; it is spun on a flat plate and the game master would cover it up immediately with a bowl before it fell flat and people bet on the number that they think is going to come up. They played and gambled at our home whilst I looked on. My mother could not say anything for fear that it would cause an argument.

I do not only remember the bad things about my father, we also spent good times together. When we drove in the car together, he would be so proud of me when I was able to read the shop names. He loved us, but alcohol and jealousy would make him be nasty to my mum.

My parents slept in separate rooms. I always slept with my mum because I did not like my father tickling me with the stubble of his unshaved beard.

One evening, he asked me if I would sleep with him, and as a reward, he would take me for a nice dinner at a restaurant. My favourite food was stir-fried rice with beef (called *loc lac*) or lobster. I promised that I would sleep with him. Soon after dinner we got back home, but I ran straight to my mum's bedroom. Although my father called me, I did not come out.

Due to his drinking my father became ill. He was treated at *Calmette,* an expensive French hospital. I remember visiting him on a few occasions. He was as thin as a skeleton, but his stomach was swollen like a fully pregnant woman. After the operation, the doctor told him that he was suffering from liver cancer. The doctor felt pity to see that he had a young child and suggested that we take my father home to save money since he was dying and could no longer be treated anyway.

My mother never told me how she felt at the time. She decided to take my father home so he could spend his last days with the family. We had Buddhist priests, monks, and relatives come to pray. Photographs taken at the time have not survived, thought I was only six years old, I remember it all.

My father's funeral took place at our house in Phnom Penh. In the Buddhist religion, if a parent dies, all children must wear white clothes and one of the sons in the family must have his head shaved in order to show respect for the departed. So, I had my hair shaved, wore white clothes, and became a novice monk on the day of the funeral. After a few days, the priests and monks took my father's coffin on a procession for cremation to *Wat Botumvatey*, a Buddhist temple. The elders were sitting around my mother to comfort her. I sat next to the monks by the coffin where they kept chanting. Many other people were walking behind the procession beside my mum, family, and friends.

When it was dark, they started the cremation. I could see the fire and smoke about 30 meters away and decided to have a look. I could see my father's body on a pile of logs with the flames burning him. The caretaker had a long stick in his hands, with which he kept prodding my father's skull. I stood there watching but did not feel anything emotionally. I was watching and catching crickets at the same time.

The next morning, we went to collect his bones. My mother and all our relatives gathered to put his remains in a small basket and then washed the remains with pure coconut water.

A few days later, I went back to school. At the time, I did not feel sad nor did I miss my father, but I do remember that I cried when the priest shaved my head. Apart from that, I was busy with my cousins who were the same age as me. One of them said to me, "It was so much fun at your dad's funeral, with plenty of drinks like Cola Cola. I wish my dad died too. So, I can enjoy it." He was a year older than me.

My mother carried on working and took care of the business as best she could. Sadly, our relatives soon seemed to have forgotten about us and the ones who did not forget tried to take advantage of us. My mother's sister in-law, the wife of Prak Chhorn, tried to force my mum to close her business and leave her shop by putting up the rent. She was not kind to my mum, but Prak Chhorn, my father's brother, was.

I do not remember any of my cousins coming to visit me, but maybe I was too busy with my school, or perhaps I was too young to pay much attention.

2

Ten years later my mother remarried.

One fine day, I was sitting in the front showroom of our shop together with my mum and grandmother. A man called Pen Em arrived on his Mobilet motorbike. He was pleasantly surprised to see my mother who introduced him to my grandmother, but only as a friend. They chatted about family and found out that he was in the process of divorcing his wife. It was only a short visit as he had just spotted my mother from the road and popped in to say hello. He used to chat with her while his wife was sat in a *cyclo*, a taxi bike, waiting for him.

He kept coming to visit us and spend time with us after work. I liked him and started to call him uncle. Many weeks or perhaps months later, he asked my mother to marry him. Initially, she refused because he was younger than she was and her older brother did not approve of the marriage, as he felt that Pen Em was looking for a rich widower. But the man persisted in his pursuit and went to ask my grandmother's permission who welcomed the idea. She believed that Pen Em was a nice man and did not want any gossip from anyone. My mother, however, still refused to marry him.

One evening, while my mother was asleep, Pen Em told me quietly in a wobbly voice that he was going to commit suicide by jumping into the river because my mum had refused to marry him. He looked sad and started to cry.

After he left, I quickly woke my mum up and told her what he just said. We immediately jumped into the car and went to the spot by the river in front of the royal palace where we had been so many times before. There, we found his motorbike parked on the grass and my mum went to find him. Because I was sleepy, I did not join her and stayed in the car instead; I was simply too tired. The next day mother agreed to get married.

My mother and stepfather Pan Penh You & Pem Em (Din Deoun)

After the small wedding, my stepfather moved in with us. I still called him uncle because I felt that he was not my real father, but Pen

Em begged me to stop calling him uncle. If I called him 'dad' he would buy me a new bicycle. Since I badly wanted a bicycle, I agreed. He was a charming, kind, and handsome man with whom I got on well. He worked at a local military office base as an accountant. Every night after he had finished his work at the office, he would come home and help my mum with her business and me with my studies.

Soon, my mother and her new husband had two sons and a daughter. My first stepbrother, Chan Sokbonn Din, was born on Monday the 25th of April 1966 in the year of the horse, and the second, Kosal Din, on Wednesday the 17th of July 1967 in the year of the goat.

My mother longed for a daughter. She had difficulty giving birth but finally, her wish came true, and my sister Chan Bonnary Din was born on Monday the 23rd of October 1972 in the year of the rat. My mum and our whole family, were filled with joy.

My stepfather was a hardworking man, he was always helpful. However, he could also be a little tight-fisted, even though the business was going well and we were receiving orders from customers all over the country.

Together with my stepfather, we delivered Buddha statues to various temples in different provinces. One day, we went in our little Suzuki pickup to deliver Buddha statues to a temple far from the city. It was a hot day on the road, and I told my stepfather that I was hungry and thirsty. I suggested that we stop and have something to eat, but he was so worried about spending money that he said, "Wait a little further, we are nearly there, or wait till we get home," and would not buy anything to eat. When I got back, I told my mum that he was a stingy man.

Thanks to all mother's hard work and the good teamwork between her and my stepfather, she managed to purchase the property that we rented from my father's brother, paying him in full.

Many years later after my uncle had died, my mother bought more properties from his wife. Mother also bought six and half hectares of land from Mr. Ros Viv and divided it into 110 plots for sale. I saw the map of the land myself and mother reserved the best plot for her children for when we were grown up. She kept saying to me that one day we would travel to see the world.

We expanded our business by running taxis from Phnom Penh city to different provinces. We started with one taxi until we had five which were all Peugeot 404 models.

This was just a few years before Pol Pot came to power and sadly her hopes and dreams of travelling did not come true. The evil communist Khmer Rouge destroyed everything.

My Stepfather Mr. Pen Em (Din Deoun) far right. Pictures taken in his military uniform with his troop in 1972. His brother in law (Hin) stands on the right.

3

1970. Even though I was still young, I sensed that Cambodia was changing. On the day of the revolution, my school had its name changed from 'Yukanthor College' to '18th March College'. Being an area rich in rice, fish, and beautiful forests did not mean that war could not touch us.

At the time, Cambodia was a country with a population of just six million people. In 1953, King Norodom Sihanouk of Cambodia had declared independence from the French. Then, two years later, he abdicated his throne so that he could become involved with politics. Many Khmer people followed his party, The Sangkum Reastr Niyum, because they received benefits and support from him. He constructed factories, schools and encouraged irrigation to help farmers.

Our neighbouring countries were fighting. South Vietnam, with the help of the Americans, was fighting North Vietnam, as well as the South Vietnamese dissenters, the Viet Cong. The war was spreading into Cambodia because the Viet Cong troops were known to take refuge in Cambodia.

That same year, 1970, General Lon Nol and his American supporters took power from Norodom Sihanouk. I was too young to understand all the politics, however, I could still sense that the country had changed.

We used to call flared trousers *elephant legs'*. The elephant leg-style began to appear in Phnom Penh. People became westernised, our culture changed, and the Cambodians started copying everything from Thailand and Vietnam.

With Americans came dollars and with dollars came governmental corruption. Lon Nol's soldiers roamed the streets to kidnap young students like myself for the army. Rich parents were able to pay ransoms to get their sons back, whilst poor families lost theirs to the war.

On my way home from school, there was an army checkpoint that I had to dodge every day. Things were so corrupt that even at school you could pay for better results. I remember once I was in danger of failing my PE diploma. I could play sports, but I just could not climb the rope, which was part of the exam. My mother knew how the game worked and gave the teacher some money. I ended up getting my PE diploma. Nobody cared about the country, everyone was just worried about how to get rich and wanted to do so as fast as possible.

Outside Phnom Penh, there was a war going on. The Khmer Rouge, now supporters of the abdicated King Norodom Sihanouk, had escaped to the jungle but resurfaced to attack the forces of the new Khmer Republic. As an extension of the Vietnam and Cambodian Civil War, the Khmer Republic, and General Lon Nol fought alongside the Americans and the South Vietnamese. They fought against the Viet Cong and some of the Khmer Rouge forces, who were hiding in the eastern jungles and border regions of Cambodia. Soon, the victor of the jungles emerged as the Khmer Rouge.

During this time, the Americans were given falsified reports containing increased numbers of soldiers, so that the voracious commanders in the Khmer Republic would be subsidised with more money.

One of my father's eldest brothers, Pen Eam, profited from this practice. He was a high-ranking officer, above Major in Lon Nol's forces, who were funded by the Americans. In his report, he had hundreds of more soldiers under his command for whom he provided wages, equipment, and food. In fact, he only had a few hundred men in his unit. The wages went to my uncle, the food was traded at the black market and the equipment found its way to the Khmer Rouge. My uncle went to fight the Khmer Rouge. Many other powerful officers were involved in similar fraudulent schemes. There was too much corruption and too much greed, which is why General Lon Nol's forces lost the war.

Bombs were dropped on the rice fields and villages, and many refugees came to Phnom Penh. Our house was full of relatives from the countryside who had escaped from the Khmer Rouge. Instead of a full day at college, I now only went in the morning so that the students who were refugees could attend in the afternoon. It was my dream to go to university and become a doctor, so my mum paid for me to take extra courses at other private high schools.

The Khmer Rouge were getting closer to Phnom Penh destroying all the bridges and cutting off all the main national roads along the way. We were stuck in Phnom Penh and the whole city was dependent on American aid. Many civilian office workers had to join the army either voluntarily or by force. My stepfather had to join the army as his workplace was being taken over. Many college students had to train for battle and joined commando groups. Some liked the idea and were proud to wear army uniforms, but I did not want to be involved. The situation in the country was getting worse.

Increasingly, rockets began to fall close to us. I cannot forget the time a rocket hit the Toul Kork area, where the main national television aerial was situated. It was also a place where poor refugees were camping in hundreds of bamboo huts, crammed together. The rockets came during the night, the huts began to burn and since everyone was asleep, they were taken by surprise and had insufficient time to escape.

The news broke in the morning and I was curious to see what happened, so I went to Toul Kork with my cousin on his motorbike. I saw many burned bodies covered under ashes; the smoke and fumes were still burning. That night, I could not eat or for days afterwards and my food smelled of the burnt flesh that I had seen. My mother did not know that I had gone over with my cousin. But life went on.

One day, my stepfather told us that he thought we were going to lose the war to the Khmer Rouge because we kept losing battles and the Khmer Rouge had already taken over the outskirts of the city. He also said that the Americans had offered to helicopter our family out of Phnom Penh and take us to Thailand. But my mother refused to have her children leave their home, their culture, and their grandmother, saying, "I will not let the Americans take my children away, to dress them up in a different uniform and send them back to war again, this time to fight against their own nation. We have suffered long enough with this war."

Mother immediately started to prepare to get us into safety. She had a bunker built inside our house on the ground floor next to the kitchen. She placed sandbags against the walls and above the ceiling which would give us some extra protection against the rockets. We could hear the rockets being fired from across the Mekong River. I could guess if the rocket would land near us or a way off from the noise it made.

At one point, a rocket landed just a few meters from our house. We were lucky that it hit the electric cables outside our house and exploded before it reached us. Fragments of the rocket flew through my open bedroom window, went through the mosquito net, the bedroom door, and finally hit the fridge. Some rocket fragments hit the sidewall of our house. Gradually, we needed to hide in our bunker more and more. We were fortunate to live in a brick house with a solid concrete roof, rather than in a wooden house with thin tin roofs, like others.

From the 14th to the 16th of April, we celebrated the Khmer New Year for three days without the usual fireworks or parties. Instead, we listened to the gunfire and rockets as they flew over our heads. My grandmother had gone to stay at my uncle's house on the outskirts of the city for the New Year. My stepfather was on duty at his military base on the 17th of April, so he was spending the night. Myself, my little brothers, sister, and my mother were at home.

4

At dawn on the 17th of April 1975, we heard: "Get out! Get out! Get out of the house now!" The Khmer Rouge had taken over Phnom Penh, ending the Cambodian Civil War and the Khmer Republic. Instead, it brought much worse – the Cambodian Genocide.

The soldiers who were shouting were both teenagers, about my age. Both looked angry and were dressed in the evil black uniform of the Khmer Rouge with Khmer scarves (*kroma*) tied around their necks. They were carrying AK47 rifles and had hand grenades strapped to their chests.

I did not open the door but looked through the shutters as they shouted at me, "Get out of your house now, everyone! Leave the doors open and windows unlocked. Get out now or we'll shoot you." I did not dare to ask questions. Instead, I nodded and said I would. Then they left and moved to the next house.

When the Khmer Rouge soldiers hammered on our door, my mother and the four of us were having rice soup for breakfast. My stepfather was at his military base where he had to spend the night. We were unclear about what was going on in Phnom Penh.

Throughout the night we heard bombs explode, the sounds of gunfire ricocheting across the city and rockets exploding in the distance. We heard our neighbours talking loudly and everyone began to lock themselves in their houses.

Breakfast was abandoned. Mother was in shock and dismay. My grandmother was at my uncle's house, far away in another district, called Bing (lake) Japan. My mum immediately decided to get in touch with my stepfather, whose army barracks was miles away from our house. She asked our driver, whose name was Sorn, nicknamed[1] Neang, to go and fetch my father from his barracks by motorbike. She gave Neang my stepfather's civilian clothes to put on. If the Khmer Rouge caught him in his army uniform, he would be executed.

Neang went off in a hurry. I cannot remember how long it took him to get my stepfather, but it seemed like a very long time. Everyone was worried and did not know what to do: should we leave our house or stay put?

As fast as we could, we started to pack some clothes, collect her valuable jewellery that was stored in the cabinet, and gather the money we had hidden in various places in the house. We left the deeds to our land, our house, and our businesses in the cabinet. Though we knew little about the situation and the position of the Khmer Rouge, my mother had prepared a little should this day come. She had tailored her *sarong* (a long skirt that all Khmer women wear at home) and had sewn inside four deep pockets in which she put her jewels, her gold, and her precious stones.

After a while, Neang returned with my father, which was a huge relief to us. My dad decided we should leave as soon as possible, so we started to pack everything we needed: some rice, baby food for my sister, clothes, blankets, and mosquito nets.

We packed everything into our four-wheel drive. My mother asked Neang to look after the house and told him to take anything he wanted to his family. I left my precious motorbikes inside the front of the house. I rode the Honda PC every day but had never used my gold orange-coloured Yamaha since I wanted to keep it new.

We all left the house in a panic and drove to my uncle's house on the west side of town. Lots of people had started moving out of their houses. On the road were people on their motorbikes, bicycles, and even walking with their belongings on their shoulders or balanced on the top of their heads. All the shops were closed. Some shops and houses were abandoned in haste and had their doors wide open. Others were darkened and charred from the night before.

The Khmer Rouge soldiers were driving around in tanks and green Chinese army trucks fired their guns into the air, telling us to get out of the city. The situation was tense; everyone was in a rush, with frightened faces. No-one stopped to chat, no groups gathered as they would normally do.

We parked the car inside the gate of my uncle's house. My cousins had already arrived. From the morning until afternoon more relatives kept showing up. My uncle, You Sambath, nicknamed Mot, arrived at the house accompanied by his wife, their three children, and grandmother along with two more families and their children. Everyone did what they could to organise food and find places to sleep that night.

Together, we discussed the situation and came up with a plan of action.

I talked to my closest cousin You Sam Eoun or Ngoy, who was two years older than me. We went to the same college and we always hung out together in our spare time. At one point we fell out because I passed my diploma whereas he failed. Because of this, he felt embarrassed and had been avoiding since then, but fortunately, we had started talking again recently. I asked him if he could take me back to my house on his motorbike to get some of my belongings.

We left without anyone noticing. We rode the motorbike across small roads, cutting through side streets to avoid the crowded routes to my house. I went around the back and noticed that it had not yet been looted. I picked up some books and some of my clothes from my room. We also assembled all the family silver and hid it in the ceiling under the roof where my mother had created a secret hiding place.

My dog followed me around the house. She had long white fur like a Scottie dog. I felt so sad to hear her whining. It seemed like she was begging me not to leave her. "Dilla, stay here safe and sound. I will be coming back in a day or so."

I was close to tears as I put out some food for her, cooked rice, fish, water, and anything I could find. We had to leave as quickly as we could. I never saw my lovely Dilla again.

We went back to join our family. Nobody, except the toddlers and babies slept that first night. Since the electricity and water supply had been cut off, we used candles and torches to find our way around the house. When the night came and it was getting dark, my father and three of my uncles helped each other to dig a few holes by the coconut trees in the back garden.

There they buried important things that might have caused us trouble if we were found with them. Their digging quickened with the sound of nearby gunfire and the glow of fires burning in the distance. There was no news on the radio, as it had been taken over by the Pol Pot guerrillas. We continued to fill the cars with our belongings and that night we cried and prayed.

---

1. In Cambodia, we hardly ever call people by their real names and had nicknames or terms of endearment for everyone. In my case, my friends, neighbours, and teachers all called me Houch or Neang. *Houch* means whistling because when I was a baby, I used to form my mouth to make a puckered O shape, as if I were whistling. And *Neang* simply means dear boy or girl.

5

Armed with guns, grenades, and rocket launchers swung over their shoulders, more Khmer Rouge soldiers entered Phnom Penh the next day at dawn. They wore a black uniform, Chinese-style hats, *kroma* scarves around their necks, and had hateful, angry expressions on their faces. With their rocket launchers and guns pointing at us, they ordered us to leave immediately. If we did not move as quickly as they wanted us to, they would fire their guns in the air. We were terrified and followed their orders in disbelief of what was happening around us.

The Khmer Rouge soldiers continuously referred to us as 'comrades' and told us that the Americans were going to drop bombs on Phnom Penh. According to them, it would be safer to leave Phnom Penh, and that we needed to go to the countryside. "Comrades, you will be back to your homes in two or three days," they promised.

We had no choice, and simply had to believe them. My uncle was the first to move his car out of the house, leading the way. Martin and Rene, his two German Shepherd dogs, were squeezed tightly into the back of his car. He loved his dogs dearly and could not abandon them. I thought of Dilla and felt very sad about abandoning her.

We started to move our cars slowly until we reached the junction which joined the main road. I could not believe what I was witnessing. The road was absolutely packed with cars, motorbikes, bicycles, wheelchairs, and push carts with bicycle wheels. Amongst them was a scattering of people of all ages, clutching onto their belongings: families, elderly people, teenagers, toddlers, and babies. Some were praying, some were crying, and others were cursing to themselves quietly.

Each of us inched forward, all headed in the same direction, to the same unknown destination. Already the tide of people was tired and frightened, and many had tears in their eyes. We could not stop to ask what was happening or even talk to anybody. Meanwhile, we kept hearing gunshots and the Khmer Rouge soldiers were constantly shouting at us to keep moving. If we did not keep moving, it was clear what would happen.

Everyone continued along on the road, all the while the Khmer Rouge soldiers looked down on us in loathing. Some of the soldiers were even younger than me; I guessed that the youngest were thirteen years old. Not yet their full height, the end of their guns dragging along the floor.

It was clear that they hated us – it was written across their faces. They looked proud of themselves that they could control us with the ease of rounding up animals. Some of them had a radio strapped over their shoulders with the loud sound of Khmer Rouge songs or Chinese-style music. They must have relished in watching the devastating scene.

Many of the young Khmer Rouge had been recruited as supporters of Sihanouk, and apolitical peasants. They fought for him and had very little understanding of Communism.

It is estimated that tens of thousands of youths were used in the Khmer Rouge's deadly regime. The youth (especially those from lower social classes) were a fundamental drive for implementing the revolution. They were uneducated, angry, and their young minds were mouldable to Pol Pot's ideology.

Literacy rates remained low within the Khmer forces and indoctrination and military training were prioritised. In fact, this was preferred as illiteracy meant they could not reach out and understand other ideas –complete and thorough indoctrination was more effective this way.

* * *

We had left the house early that morning at around 6 am when it was still cool and bearable. It was April and in Cambodia, which is often dry and without rain, it is the hottest month of the year. By midday we were exhausted and we could feel the dry heat sitting on top of us. Yet, we had not moved far at all, maybe five or six hundred metres from the house.

On both sides of the main road were high buildings. On the ground floors were shops, cinemas, restaurants, pharmacies. Above, on the first and second floors were residential flats. All the shops had been broken into, most of them were left open and some were blackened from being set alight.

I just kept pushing the car together with my father whilst my mother sat inside and steered as we crept along. My grandmother, sister, and two brothers were sitting behind her. My sister who was only three years old was crying and needed milk.

By the afternoon, we were on the road to the Kbal Thnal bridge. Along that road were large houses with high walls, gates, and beautiful villas along with important government buildings including the American Embassy.

As we passed the gates of the embassy, amongst a group of people I saw dead bodies, some of whom were wearing army and police uniforms. They must have been killed the night before. Flies hovered over their bodies. Some appeared to be still alive but had blood on their garments. Others had bandages on their bodies, drips attached to their arms, or were in hospital wheelchairs.

I heard someone mutter that the Khmer Rouge had forced all the patients out of the local hospitals. Several families pushed their relatives on their hospital beds, wooden carts, or bicycles, still dressed in their thin hospital gowns. The teenage Khmer Rouge soldiers sneered as they were wheeled by.

I was thirsty but had no appetite, feeling numb and sad. No one knew what was going to happen next, or where we were heading. We were close to the roundabout near to the bridge, the shuffling pace of the exodus had come to a halt.

Something was happening nearby and we heard cries and screams for mercy. The screams were coming from my uncle's sister-in-law, Ley. She was begging the Khmer rouge soldiers to free her son, who looked very young, eighteen or maybe twenty. He had been caught wearing a commando uniform, which every college student was given to be able to join the cadets. It did not mean that he was in the army.

When I passed by, I caught a glimpse of him with his arms tied behind his back as he was dragged away. We would never know what happened to him. The soldiers shouted and pointed their weapons at Aunt Ley and shouted at her to be quiet or else they would shoot. She had to stop crying and let them take her son away. There was nothing we could do to help, we had to keep quiet. People had been arrested because they had army possessions and were accused of being soldiers or spies. We now feared for our own safety because we had some army items too.

A few of the items that we had with us, like our mosquito nets, blankets, and some of the cups and water bottles, were army equipment. So, we discreetly dropped them underneath our car as we were inching along. Many people around us did the same.

Moving slowly with our car, we were not allowed to stop to drink or eat, not that we felt hungry. At that moment, I heard a woman cry in pain and saw a pregnant woman behind us sitting on a bicycle that her husband was pulling. She was going into labour. Her husband begged everyone around him to help her. Luckily, my uncle You Ol was a doctor, and he told the man to put her in the back of our car. We let her lie down and my uncle delivered the baby in our car. She gave birth safely and cried with joy. Both were grateful and gave thanks to my uncle and carried on moving with their new-born baby.

The heat of the sun made the atmosphere unbearable. The sky was so clear, there were no clouds to help block the sun and give us some shade. Just as the heat of the glaring sun, there was no escape from the gaze of the Khmer Rouge soldiers.

Occasionally, some of them became suspicious or bored. If they found a person or family who looked suspicious then that person was searched. They would stop a family and search them, taking delight in brutally spilling a family's belongings on the road. If they found anything, like army uniforms, identity cards, or equipment, the soldiers simply dragged the person over to the side of the road, shot them, and resumed their close vigil.

Shockingly, this would become the norm.

I remember the smell of burning houses. Even though the sound of gunfire was no longer new, I was scared every time I heard it. I worried about what would become of us but being with my family helped me to have the energy to stand and keep pushing the car.

We were with four other families walking together with seven old ladies, including my grandmother. Those old ladies were dressed like nuns and wore white blouses. They were Buddhists and had their heads shaved to show their devotion to their beliefs. They did not say anything but continued to whisper their prayers. My mind drifted back a few months to the day my mum, her sister-in-law, and the nuns prepared a special Buddhism ceremony.

The purpose of the Buddhism ceremony was intended to pray for peace. It was the crowning of a large Buddha statue specially made from our shop. The statue had glass eyes and a precious stone placed on his forehead between his eyebrows. It was an exciting occasion and I remember how thrilled I was as the nuns arranged small triangular flags, coloured red and yellow around the statue. These flags were symbolic of peace and safety and were adorned with pictures of Buddha and inscribed with words from the Pali language. The old ladies had brought the small flags with them when we left the house.

However, after we saw what the soldiers did with those who had any suspicious items, the group of old ladies decided to quietly discard the flags on the ground under the cars. This went unnoticed and they went on whispering their prayers for safety and to return home. As if someone had heard their pleas, after they discarded the flags with respect, the sky turned cloudy. We continued to walk quietly with our heads down.

Under the Khmer Rouge, all monks were disrobed, there were no monks or religion from 1975 to 1979. Some monks were prosecuted if they refused to give up their lifestyle.

That night we had rain pouring heavily. It was a miracle we were all still alive.

We spent our first night on the road with many other people. Whilst my grandmother, sister, brothers, and my mother slept in the car, my father and I lay on a mat underneath it. The car was a four-wheel-drive model, meaning that the car was high off the ground. All of us went to sleep with empty stomachs, but I did not feel at all hungry.

In the middle of the night, I woke up to the sound of thunder and rain which was pouring down heavily. It was so much so I could feel the water running under my back, but amongst all the other horrors it did not bother me, and I went back to sleep. The day-long walk had exhausted me, and I quickly fell back into a deep sleep.

We started our walk again before sunrise, whilst it was still cool. We got as far as to cross a bridge to the east side of the Mekong River, and we spent our second night there.

My uncle's family had a friend who lived close to the area, and we were curious to find out if he was still there. His house was big and made of wood and was slanted on the ground. I went in with my mother, but it was empty, and the door was unlocked. Nobody was there. We searched the house, moving from room to room and collected what we needed. We managed to salvage some mosquito nets, blankets, cooking pots, spoons, salt, and some rice. Although we did not want to take it, we needed to survive.

We cooked some rice, using anything we could, and had our dinner on the street. Some people used the hubcaps from abandoned cars to cook food, any containers or any pieces of metal would do. I cannot remember what we had for dinner that night, perhaps just rice, and salt. I also cannot recall if we washed or what we used for a toilet, but I remember we assigned the riverbank for sanitary use. The whole area was deserted; the houses were emptied and the only thing that inhabited the neighbourhood was a horrible burning smell.

We could hear communist songs drifting through the air, spat out by a Khmer Rouge radio. We were in total darkness; there were no lights or sounds except children's cries in the distance and the occasional menacing blasts of gunshots. I did not speak to any of my family nor my cousins. I just sat alone in a veil of sadness.

That evening, I sat on the curb on the corner of the street with a pile of books that I had rescued from my home. I sat facing the west side of the river. Flicking in the far distance, I could see some shining neon lights. Tears in my eyes, I imagined my home. I missed my school, my friends, and my house. Lost and alone, I just sat on top of my books crying and speaking to no one. I was wondering when we would next see our home.

I had to abandon all my books. Some people were using books, sheets of paper, or bank notes as toilet paper or for rolling tobacco. Money had no value, and it became apparent to those who had money, that it was useless. There were no shops, or markets and anyone who was interested in money. Instead, we bartered gold, diamonds, clothes, and watches for food.

The Khmer Rouge forced us at gunpoint to move on the next morning. Our attempts to delay and stay close to Phnom Penh were failing. They kept forcing us onwards, eastwards, towards the direction to the Vietnamese border and away from Phnom Penh. Not many people passed us in the other direction.

None of us knew where we were going or where we could stay. But, under the strict gaze of the soldiers, we kept inching forward, following the group of people in front of us. They were pushing their cars, bicycles, and make-shift carts that they had fashioned with an old bike and car wheels. We saw many cars abandoned on the road, even luxury cars like Mercedes. They had been vandalized, the wheels were taken off and the tires slashed. All that was left was an abandoned metal skeleton. Along the way, people searched and scavenged for anything that would help make things a little easier – food, vegetables, anything we could make use of. We needed to save diesel for our car, so we continued to push it.

The Khmer Rouge soldiers kept looking at us and calling us capitalists, which to them was an insult. In their eyes, we were different, to be scorned and hated.

They did not care about us or even see us as people and they certainly had no sympathy for our animals. It was not safe for us to have our two beautiful dogs with us. The whole family was upset when my uncle made the devastating decision to leave his dogs, Martin, and René. Both dogs looked ill; they were exhausted and although they would drink water, they would not eat. We had to leave them alongside the road. They were sorrowful and whining, but they did not want to follow us. We said our sad goodbyes to them and moved on.

We walked a small distance and stopped again when it got dark. It was not possible to wash because there was no water. While our parents were busy setting up camp for the night, my cousin and I went back to the place where we left Martin and René because we were missing them so much. It was dark now, but I imagined that they would still be lying on the ground, where we had left them. The smell of the campfires dotted around the people-filled area, and the sound of children crying in the distance filled our senses.

As we got to the place where we had left them that morning, we saw a small fire, used for cooking where people were barbecuing an animal on a spit. The creature was shaped like a dog. We could not find our Martin and René. I still have the image burning in my eyes. I hoped that the animal on the spit was not Martin or René, but we never found out where they disappeared to.

We returned to our camp without saying a word to our family. We did not want to upset them.

6

The stench of human waste. Dead bodies were putrefied and bloated from the heat of the day lay on the ground next to the road. Few people noticed. There were hordes of people on the roads and people in the fields, but there was no room to move. We found some water from a well and picked vegetables that we found on an abandoned farm. With the few possessions and valuables that we had been able to carry, we tried to barter with locals for the essential food that we desperately needed. By now most of the travellers began to get diarrhoea and many of the younger children developed fevers.

Along the way, we came across a few of our friends and neighbours that we knew from Phnom Penh. Some said that they planned to go back to their birthplaces on the farm or were going to stay with relatives in the countryside in different provinces. This was not an option for us as our relatives lived hundreds of miles away.

My father and our uncles decided that we should keep moving towards Kien Svay village in Kandal province. It was a popular place where people from Phnom Penh spent their weekends or had picnics with their children and families. Before the war, it had been a lovely spot with emerald green lakes. I used to ride my motorbike with my college friends to play football at the weekend.

By now, I had lost count of the number of days that we had been on the road. There was no water because it was the dry season and the April days were swelteringly hot. It was getting harder and harder every day. Our food supplies were nearly gone. We were still bartering anything we had for rice that we could mix with vegetables, which went some way to filling our stomachs. We knew that our valuables would soon be exhausted. We had nothing, apart from rice and salt.

One afternoon, after many days of walking, we reached a place that was packed full of people, families, children, and cars. The people were gathered around a temple called *Wat Cham Puss Ka Eak*. Before it had been a serene oasis, full of trees, and many rows of buildings built for the monks, who were now gone. The temple had large grounds, which accommodated us for a while. Next to the main temple hall was a large deep pond full of clear cool water. There was lotus growing inside the pond with flowers and lotus fruits.

I was so pleased to see water and we carried handfuls of it out from the pond and washed ourselves at the edge. It was late afternoon with a strong wind, rain clouds crossed the sky. It was a moment to savour. While I was washing, I suddenly felt a chill, I became cold and started shaking and trembling. My whole body was in shock and I felt that I could not breathe. My mum was standing next to me and she wrapped a towel around me. A few minutes later I was fine.

Many more people came and soon the temple was full. Everywhere we went it seemed that there were Khmer Rouge soldiers blending in with us, we were not left alone even for a minute. They kept shooting in the air and shouting at people to keep moving, telling us that we were not allowed to stay in a certain place anymore and that everyone had to move on to their villages. By this point we no longer cared; we had had enough, we needed to eat and rest.

I remember that my mum and the rest of us picked a space on the first floor of the temple building. It was an empty room about four meters squared which we shared with many family members. We used a thin blanket as a mattress. My father and uncles slept in the cars to guard our possessions.

All five of us slept in the mosquito net, which we were lucky to have because the place was swamped with mosquitos. We could hear them flying around our ears, still managing to bite us. Some people and children started to get malaria and fever. There were no lights, candles, or torches, so we made fires to light the place. Apart from the mosquitoes, and crickets, silence surrounded us.

Early the next morning, one of my uncles, Hin, his wife, and my stepfather's older sister, Pol, and his family decided to split up from us. He wanted to return to his village in the Takeo province which was my father's birthplace. Takeo is on the southern side of the country, close to the Vietnamese border. It was miles away from where we were.

My father talked with my mother, discussing if we should go with them. It would have meant splitting our family up, and my mum leaving my grandmother and her two brothers with their families. It was heart-breaking. We had no idea what would happen next. Would we see each other again? My father decided not to leave and to stay with us.

We all said farewell and my uncle's family went off early in the morning. We were deeply saddened and cried, realising that we would not see them again.

Indeed, not following my uncle to Takeo had been the right decision. We later found out that many of the people from Phnom Penh who returned to their birthplaces did not survive. When they arrived at their villages, they were interrogated by the Pol Pot soldiers. Their real identities were exposed by the villagers who knew them as city dwellers, and they were reported to Angkar (the Khmer Rouge).

Angkar believed that peasants suffered from having to loan money to city folk as opposed to property-owners or other sources of exploitation. Therefore, they justified dragging urban residents away from their home, under the assumption that it would eradicate all debt. 'New people' or city-dwellers were seen to be rich, abusive, and remnants of the old regime.

As punishment, they separated men from the families, either to execute them or send them to hard-labour camps. A labour camp was like a death sentence. Some families, like my uncle Pen Eam, his wife, son, and daughter, were so unfortunate that they were all executed together.

Pen Eam's family lived in the Kratie province. Before, he was commander-in-chief in Lon Nol's army. When the Khmer Rouge took control, he abandoned his regiment, disguised as a civilian. Shortly after splitting up from us and arriving in Sré Ronong, a village in the Takeo province, together with his wife, seventeen-year-old son, and sixteen-year-old daughter, someone in the village recognised him. They knew about his background and immediately reported him to Angkar.

Unexpectedly, the family were interrogated and searched by the Khmer Rouge soldiers who discovered their gold and jewels. They were tied up and taken away in an ox's cart. I was told that people could hear their children scream in pain from a long way away. Uncle Pen Eam had been executed alongside his family. They were slaughtered like animals and their bodies were dropped in a deep pit.

I was overwhelmed to hear this horrible news after 1982 from a cousin from Uncle Hin's family. Uncle Hin was also executed, but his wife and children survived to tell the story.

We were forced out from Wat Slaket the next day and moved on again. The rows of refugees all trudged slowly along the main national road until we stopped at another temple called Wat Champa. A classroom in the temple served as bedroom for us and six other families, but we could not mingle because it was dangerous to speak to people that we did not know. Anything that gave us away as being connected with the Khmer Republic army would be fatal – no one could know who we were. However, we stayed in Wat Champa and settled into a routine.

A large river ran from the Mekong, located about 500 meters behind the temple, and everyone bathed and washed their clothes in it. The riverbanks were steep, slippery, and deep with clay and the water was muddy yellow.

One day my mother carried my little sister to have a bath. She slipped in the water not knowing how to swim. Luckily, Sokbonn, my second younger brother, reached out his hand and pulled her to the bank. I was not present when this happened – they told me afterwards. I could not swim either at that time.

The days became repetitive. Every day, it was my job to collect drinking water from the murky river. The water was not clean enough to drink, with people urinating and washing their clothes in the same river, so the water had to be boiled first. Every so often we noticed a body floating past. Inevitably, many of us had to live with unclean water and its consequences.

At nightfall, the darkness shrouded us. Without electricity, the only light we had was from the moon and the stars. There were no sounds other than the drone of mosquitoes as they swooped to devour us, the chirping of crickets and croaking of frogs, loud and unceasing as if to entertain us. Every night, I sunk into despair, terribly missing my home and school. I dreamt about food, my empty stomach rumbling. Toddlers and babies suffered the most with malaria, fever, and diarrhoea.

One old thin lady used her car for shelter and lived alone, parked by the main road. She regularly sat on the ground next to her cream-coloured Mercedes, but I never spoke or talked to her. I walked by her almost every day to search for edible plants which I would pick off the ground, even if it were near human dung. Without a doubt, the old lady must once have been rich but now, quite alone, resigned herself to death, however it would come.

Some people still wore earrings, bracelets, and watches or even colourful clothes. They did not realise that they would be noticed and targeted by the Khmer Rouge. When the soldiers saw discernible ex-city dwellers, they assumed that they were capitalists, flaunting their wealth. This was used as evidence for the decadence of capitalists and enraged the Khmer Rouge. Soon enough the jewellery and watches would be gone. The soldiers demanded watches or jewellery at gunpoint. The communists preached their mantras to us: 'Everyone is equal', 'No rich, no poor, no capitalists'. Nevertheless, this did not stop them from taking and keeping our possessions, especially watches, fountain pens and radios.

One morning, when I was standing by the direct route leading from Phnom Penh to Svay Rieng province that went on to Vietnam, I saw a convoy of Khmer Rouge trucks with canvas roofs. They had not secured the canvas properly as some of them were flapped open to show what was inside. I stood still and watched the convoys passing one by one. Every one of the convoys was filled with electrical goods like fans, and fridges and televisions. All these goods must have been looted from the shops and people's houses in the city. Frequently, cars were transported out from Phnom Penh. I saw this everyday so reasoned that they must have been emptying the whole city of any valuable goods.

The head of each family was questioned by the Khmer Rouge soldiers and asked to provide their background and history. We were warned to tell the truth about our identities. They said that if we were well-educated and qualified with skills, we might be selected to go back to Phnom Penh earlier than anyone else. My father and uncles discussed the issue in-depth and decided to watch other families first.

Every morning, the heads of various families were called for a meeting under the tree. Those meetings would last for hours. Among us were movie stars, doctors, singers, bankers, teachers, and many educated people. We sat on the ground and listened to the Khmer Rouge preaching, calling us comrade this and comrade that.

They told us that everyone was equal, with no one having any title or status. Most of the Khmer Rouge soldiers delivering these lectures were just young teenagers. Many of them were peasants and illiterate, which we knew because when they confiscated any documents from people, they often read them upside down. Every meeting was the same monotonous drone about Angkar's policies, their victories, and how they destroyed the enemies. They repeatedly mentioned capitalists and Americans.

Wat Champa temple was our temporary home for many days. Gradually, educated men with high qualifications and skills came forward to declare themselves to Angkar. Often, they were sent away in a small car. If there were many of them, they were sent in army trucks while their wives and children were left behind waiting. Partings had to be emotionless as the Khmer Rouge soldiers were a ubiquitous, torturing presence. All we could do was hope for a miracle and to go back home.

We decided against coming forward. A few days later, everyone was told to leave Champa temple. We were told to move on to our villages or to go to another place. If we refused, our rice ration would be removed, and we would starve. So, we had no choice but to gather our belongings, pack them into our cars, and push them onto the road once more. We made our way to a village called Chan Lok, a village a few kilometres further on.

When we arrived in Chan Lok, we were told to live with a family: a husband, wife, and their son. They were uneducated farmers who grew corn, tobacco, rice, and many things depending on the season. The family lived in a wooden house with a palm leaf roof. It was built on stilts high off the ground to prevent the house from being flooded during the raining season. Under their house, they kept two oxen and an ox cart. We did not know them, but the wife introduced herself as Yong, her husband as Chhum, and their son as A Cheoum.

The family in Chan Lok clearly had something in mind for us as soon as they saw us, especially A Cheoum. A few weeks later he declared that he wanted to have one of the daughters of my Aunt Horm Sopheoun as wife.

Apparently, Chhum's family were related to Nov, one of my uncle's wives, a vegetable farmer with five children. We had one of their children, eleven-year-old Sakhonn, to stay with us, to look after my grandmother. We sent her to school and took care of her. My uncle You Mean or Mate, and her father, died just before Pol Pot came. He was an alcoholic, troublemaker, and very unpopular in the family. He had brought shame to my mother. Drunk, crying and begging for money, he had created terrible scenes in front of our house. Our neighbours had heard and witnessed his bad behaviour. He even stole my new bicycle that I left in front of the house which was given to me by my stepfather. I was too young to say anything, but I was very upset. None of the family wanted to know him except my mother.

We had to depend on Aunt Nov's relatives, the Chhum family, to let us take refuge on their premises. Three other families were also staying with them. In total, there were twenty-nine of us. Their house was completely overcrowded. Some of us had to sleep in the car and under the trees. We even made tents from plastic sheets to create more space. Sometimes at night, it was raining with strong winds, it would be so loud that we would sit up from our sleep. The six of us in my family shared a small bamboo deck under a tree at the front of their house. Using the deck to both eat and sleep, there was no privacy. We stayed there for several weeks.

7

The Khmer Rouge let us settle into our new living arrangements, taking note of our identities and interrogated us yet again about our family history. They told us that we had better be honest and tell them where we came from and what jobs we had done before the Khmer Rouge had taken over. Our compliance and honesty were of the utmost importance because if we did not have the necessary skills to aid the regime, Angkar would need to send us back to Phnom Penh to retrain.

The Khmer Rouge said that if anyone came forward or volunteered, Angkar would take care of their families while the men were away. They claimed that it would only be for a short period, about three months. However, we did not trust them and were fearful of the real consequences.

As we suspected, these were all just terrible lies.

The families discussed what to do amongst themselves. Should we send our husbands away or keep quiet? Either option seemed daunting.

At home, the situation seemed to be turning from bad to worse as we had started to run out of food. We had to exchange the rest of our personal belongings like watches, clothes, gold for rice, sugar, salt, corn, anything to keep us alive. The dire circumstances meant that the four families, still living in such close quarters, constantly argued, disagreed, and were unhappy.

It got so bad that my mother and stepfather began to think that the best option was to let him declare his identity.

One day, we heard through the grapevine that there were many fish in the holes left by American's bombs dropped from their B52 warplanes. These holes were scattered throughout the fields.

My stepfather, uncle Mot, and I left home early in the morning and walked across the fields to find the place where the bombs had been dropped and went to try and catch fish. The rumours were true and we found a hole around three or four meters in diameter, one metre deep with some water and lotus growing inside. Amongst the long grass and small bushes, the hole looked like a shallow pond. There was no sign of the Khmer Rouge, which was good because we would not know what to say if they caught us.

We got straight to work. My stepfather and uncle used mud to build a dyke, separating the pond into two parts. Then all of us used buckets to pour water from one side of the pond to the other. When the water level on one side was lower, we could see many fish crawling in the mud. Now in sight, we caught them easily from the shallow half. Then we drained the water and repeated the technique on the other side.

My uncle and I had never done this before, so my stepfather led the operation. He was raised in a rice farmer's family and had much experience in this kind of thing. We were so pleased with the amount of fish we caught – there were all sorts, even some catfish. We used lotus leaves as plates and made a fire to cook the fish, having our lunch at the edge of the pond, like a picnic. The fish was sweet and delicious, but all the while our thoughts were with our family back at home. I could not wait to go back to show them what we had caught, so much so that I was not even tired for the return journey.

That evening we shared the fish with our relatives. My stepfather asked me to cook some nice fluffy rice so he could enjoy it with the fish, but accidentally I overcooked the rice until it was soft like porridge. It was my mistake, as I thought cooking the rice that way would add volume and there would be more to go around. My stepfather was very angry with me and he told me off, saying, "All I asked was for you to cook some rice for me, but you couldn't even do that properly."

He never told me off before and that was the first time he shouted at me. My mother was unhappy with my stepfather and they had a quiet argument. She told him to declare himself to Angkar so that we all might have the opportunity to go back home.

That night, it was dark, windy, and rainy and we could not sleep because the rain was spraying all over us. My stepfather said he wanted to speak with me. We went to a corner and talked quietly, away from everyone else. He had decided to tell the Khmer Rouge that he had been in the army.

He handed me his gold necklace with many Buddha pendants. He told me to keep it safe and said, "from now on, it is your responsibility to look after the family instead of me." I replied by saying yes. His voice was trembling – he was crying. I did not say much but was very sad and hoped that he would return. I took the necklace and kept it in my pocket.

Of all the moments that I remember from this period, I hold that one in sharp focus, even today. All my uncles and my two male cousins were truthful and told the Khmer Rouge soldiers about their old professions. Amongst them, they were doctors, bankers, soldiers, and students. They told them because they believed that there would be a chance that they would be selected to go back home. We all feared that sooner or later the Khmer Rouge might find out anyway, and they would be taken away. My father, three uncles, and two teenage cousins were taken away on Tuesday 27th May 1975. They never came back.

While we were waiting for our father's return, we were forced to work in the village. I had been selected along with all my cousins to work in cornfields, rice and sugar cane fields, and tobacco farms. We had never done this kind of work before, but no one would dare to refuse Angkar. We had no skills compared to the local farmers.

Many days and weeks went by and when the raining season arrived, all the farmlands were flooded. Water came right close to the edge of the house.

Every morning, I had to get in a small boat full of men and women to cross the flooded fields to work at higher grounds. We were told to pick corn, tobacco leaves, or collect grass. I was always worried that if the boat sank, I would not survive as at the time I could not swim.

By working all day with the farmers in the village I gained some valuable experience of hard labour which, in turn, taught me how to survive. When we were in Phnom Penh, the countryside was a retreat where we adored spending our weekends and spare time, enjoying the lakes and rivers. Unfortunately, this was not the countryside leisure that we once knew.

8

Two months had passed. One day, the Khmer Rouge soldiers had exciting news for us: we were going to re-join our stepfather in Phnom Penh. We were so excited that we were overwhelmed by tears of joy.

They told us to prepare and pack our belongings, ready for the convoy that would take us back home and we felt that we had been resurrected. We said goodbye to the villagers with tears, they were upset to see us leave. My mother gave a small bracelet as a present to one of the neighbour's daughters and gave another daughter a gold watch because they had been so kind and had given us food. We felt that we would not need it as we would have everything we needed back at home.

Some of the villagers told us that we were being lied to. Instead, they said, the Khmer Rouge were going to take us to fill the jungles. We refused to believe it even though the Khmer Rouge had lied to us before. The news had to be true, they could not leave the city of Phnom Penh empty forever.

My grandmother was the most shocked by the rumour. Before we left, she said that she needed to use the toilet and walked around the back of the house, it was about fifteen meters toward the bushes between banana trees.

After a while, I heard her calling my name in panic. I ran to find my grandmother sat on the ground. She was not able to push herself up on her own. The stress from the shocking rumours must have caused her to have a small stroke and paralysed her lower body. Mum and I lifted her by her arms, carried her back to the house, and continued to pack our belongings, without a word. My mother did not say anything, nor did she show me any signs of sadness.

When the evacuation day arrived, we pushed our cart out of the village towards the meeting place along with our other relatives and many other families. A line of lorries parked in a row was waiting for us. My grandmother, my sister, and Kosal, my younger brother were sitting in the pushcart. Kosal had contracted polio when he was three years old and could not walk. It affected him in his left foot which caused his leg muscles to wilt. My heart broke; we had our grandmother, a baby sister, and a disabled brother to look after. My second brother, Sokbonn, was seven years old and managed to help us as much he could, along with my aunts and cousins. Every family who had relatives taken away for 're-education' were called to join the convoy. None of the teenage cousins from my uncle's family came to help us.

It was midmorning by the time we reached the trucks. The Khmer Rouge forced us onto the lorries with blows and curses. We were separated from our aunts and cousins and I did not have time to find any of them. We were stuffed in the truck with many others. There were six families in our truck, and at least about forty people. My grandmother sat on our belongings with my sister, brothers, and my mother. Soon the children began to cry, and the old people started to whimper. They were suffocating. There was no room to move in the back of the truck. I did not have room to sit and I was standing right at the back of the truck the whole journey, clinging onto the metal bars of the truck. The truck had a canvas roof that was zipped up securely. I could not see any daylight, and no one knew where we were going. Silently, I prayed and hoped that maybe we were being taken back to Phnom Penh as we had been promised.

Soon, I was able to peek through a tiny hole in the canvas and to take breaths of fresh air. Through the hole, I was able to catch glimpses of the outside world and it looked as though we were heading back to Phnom Penh. There were landmarks that I remembered: buildings, temples, and schools. Now they were emptied, abandoned, and instead had the Pol Pot guerrillas with black uniforms sitting on guard, or on their break in hammocks.

We passed through familiar villages that I now found hard to recognise. Whole groups of inhabitants had disappeared, not even a cat or a dog was to be seen. It was a few months since we had been forced to leave our hometown and now, we returned on the same road. What I saw through that tiny hole was complete devastation.

I kept hoping, holding positive thoughts in my mind, that we were going back to Phnom Penh to meet my father and uncles. Perhaps we would see them waiting for us at our destination. Despite this, I knew that they lied to us from the start. I lost all hope when I saw what was happening along the road…

The truck travelled fast but I knew that we were driving from the east side of Phnom Penh to the west. We reached Kbal Thnol Bridge and I started recognizing the city – we were driven across the bridge and down the main road. There were differences, the garden alongside the river had been replanted with coconut and banana trees.

Soon, I lost my sense of direction and things became less and less familiar. All I knew was that we would have reached our destination in the city if we really were stopping, but we seemed to be travelling away from Phnom Penh. The others in the truck kept asking me where we were, but I could not tell them as I did not know the area and there were no signs on the road. All I could see were dead towns and villages. I knew that we were going further and further away from Phnom Penh. The further we got from the city, the more my hope faded away. They had lied to us again. It began raining heavily so I had to close the hole.

They stopped to let us to urinate and drink water from the rice fields, but soon they were back to shouting, cursing, and pushing us back into the truck.

In all the commotion, I lost my wallet with my student identification and many precious photos of my family, which I kept in my back pocket. I was very upset.

The truck did not stop again until dark. We had no idea where we were. There was no one to ask except the Khmer Rouge driver and soldiers who were escorting the truck. My grandmother was exhausted, and she began to cough up blood. Escape seemed impossible. Even if we were able to evade the guards, it would have been too difficult to move quickly with my grandmother, my little brothers, and sister.

We stopped to stay the night by the road near a pond. It was a dark evening and we needed water. I went to fetch water from the pond, but when I returned up to the truck with water, I saw something horrible: a dead, wilted body leant against the tree trunk, looking as if it had been there for a long time with the skin at the bottom of the feet yellowing. I was terrified to discover this and realized that I could be drinking water from a pond mixed with the fluids of dead bodies.

I had no choice.

That night I slept on the ground on top of a thin bag. We dotted ourselves under and around the truck to try to stay dry. All children and elderly slept in the truck with all everyone's belongings. The moonlight and stars were shining in the dark sky but there was no way of knowing where we were or the next time we would be fed.

As soon as the sun rose and lit the road we started to move again. My mum had prepared some dried rice and packed in containers so we could suck it, let it go soft, and hope that it would slowly fill our empty stomachs. Many people had not prepared anything for the journey and were beginning to suffer. We drove from the morning until midday for a break and spent nearly two days this way.

In the afternoon of the second day, we stopped at a place by some railroad tracks. Someone among us said that we were in Posat Province. We had no idea why we stopped by the rail tracks as no one told us anything, so we simply had to watch the others and follow.

My mother, grandmother, two brothers, sister, and I were still together. We had no help in moving our grandmother from place to place along with our belongings. I had no time to think or even worry, we just kept moving otherwise we would be punished. My grandmother still could not walk from when the shock had left her unexpectedly paralysed from her waist down.

The railroad tracks were hard to walk on, I had no shoes and the sharp rocks cut my feet. My mother and I had to cross our arms to make a little chair to lift my grandmother from place to place. We would move ten meters at a time and put her down. Then, we would return to collect our belongings and the rest of the family. We repeated this action again and again. My sister was very frightened and screamed and cried every time that we moved away from her.

We found an abandoned bamboo pallet to sleep on that night. There was just enough room for us to put all our belongings on and sleep on top of them. At least we were not sleeping directly on the ground.

Next to the rail tracks were rice paddy fields where we searched for wood and water to cook rice for that night. There was nothing left to eat with the rice except a few grains of salt and some dried fish. My mum cooked up some extra rice as provisions in case the Khmer Rouge moved us again without notice. We were by the side of the railway tracks for two or three days.

The searches that the Khmer Rouge soldiers carried out were frequent, but they never found our valuables. Mother hid her jewellery under her sarong, inside the cooked rice pot, or inside the salt container.

That day two female Khmer Rouge guards came to our shelter and demanded that they search us. They poked their bayonets inside our rice pot which was full of cooked rice. Thankfully, the day before my mother had moved her jewellery to the bottom of the salt container. They checked our bags and the rest, but they did not check any of our clothes. It would be a disaster if they found our hidden jewellery, as we would have nothing left to barter with for the precious food that was keeping us alive.

People died by the side of the railway tracks. Then came the rats and flies. The heat made it worse. I scavenged for herbs or vegetables that we could cook and picked some aquatic herbs called Ma Orm that we could eat raw.

After the rain came the cool fresh air. I went to find wood, but my curiosity led me to a wooden house nearby. I wondered if I could find anything useful in that house. Barefoot, I felt the cool ground and a puddle of rainwater beneath my feet. While I made my way slowly around the house I thought about my life in Phnom Penh. When would I see my home again?

The house was nice in the wooden, traditional Cambodian style; high off the ground and supported by concrete pillars. The house was empty and silent. I went under the house to search for anything that would be useful for us, but nothing was left. I did not go upstairs because I was too scared and did not want to find a dead body or to stumble upon any Khmer Rouge soldiers.

A few days later, a freight train appeared, and the guards acted as if it had arrived on time, as expected. We were told to pack our stuff and get on the train immediately. My mum and I started to pick up my grandmother, my sister, and our belongings step by step, little by little. My feet were cut and bleeding because of the sharp rocks as we carried my grandmother and our belongings.

There were no seats on the freight train, just a wooden floor with wide-open doors as the wagons were used to transport cattle. As we moved, I was hopeful that maybe, we would be going to a better place. I could not tell how many hours we were on the train, but we left the place early morning and we stopped midday at another unknown location. We were totally lost, hungry, exhausted, and dehydrated under the glaring sun.

We were forced off the train at gun point. The building looked like it used to be a small community market in a train station, but it was now empty. Many buffalos and bulls attached to carts were waiting for our arrival. We picked an available cart close to us and we helped my grandmother and little siblings climb in. I walked behind the bulls which were pulling the cart with my mother. She was carrying our belongings on her head as we all walked through the thick dust and hot sand on uneven tracks that soon turned into jungle tracks.

Instead of sharp stones lacerating my feet, we now walked on bamboo stems that cut them and hot sand that blistered them. The uneven track jolted the cart so much that we really had to keep an eye on everyone. The road was terribly bumpy, and the cart was tilted to the left and right throughout the journey. At one point, Kosal nearly had his head caught in the cart's wheel. He was unable to sit or hold onto the cart, lost his balance and his head went towards the wheel. Luckily, my mum saw it and screamed at the driver to stop the cart, which he did just before his neck was snapped in the spokes.

In complete silence, we walked deeper into the jungle, following the carts. The guards told us to stop and make a shelter. We picked a spot with some smooth ground under the shade of the small tree to make our camp and put the plastic sheet on the ground for us to sleep. There were ants and insects everywhere around us. Without food or water to sustain us my little sister cried with hunger and my grandmother looked exhausted.

I went into the forest close by to collect dead wood to make a fire even though we did not have a lighter. I broke small tree branches with my bare hands to make a shelter, and used long, soft grass and tree leaves to make the roof. Sokbonn and Kosal searched for water as best as they could whilst my grandmother tried to comfort and quieten my little sister.

Fortunately, we found a small stream hidden by the jungle. The water was yellow, and we could see dead leaves and many wild plants growing alongside the stream bank. We collected water for our mother so that she could cook rice and make drinkable water. The water had mosquitoes' lava swimming in it, but we did not care. Then, the three of us returned with a small broken mosquito net which we used as a fishing net.

I did not want to go in the water since I was afraid of the leeches. Kosal, small but brave, volunteered to go in the water to try and catch some fish. The water was stagnant, cold, yellow, and full of dead leaves. We caught a few tiny shrimps, but no fish. We also caught some water beetles and small insects, but we released them back as we could not eat them.

That first day, we mixed our rice with edible leaves and made a kind of thick soup. We added some salt just to make the flavour better. Back home we would not even feed it to a pig, but we were starving, so we had no choice. After we had eaten it, we had diarrhoea straight away.

That afternoon, the rain came, soaking us. Keeping as many of our belongings dry under the plastic sheet as possible, we sat under our leaf roof with rainwater running between the leaves and underneath us. The rain stopped as it got dark and we managed to keep the fire alight, located next to our shelter to help keep warm and keep mosquitos and wild animals away. That night we had rice soup mixed with any edible leaves that we could find in the forest. It was tasteless, but we needed to fill our stomachs.

The camp soon grew with families whose husbands had been taken away, like ours. There was Mrs Yim Pan Yee with her four children, a boy aged fourteen, and three girls aged thirteen, ten, and nine. She had a sister aged twenty named Srey. Mrs Yim Pan Yee's husband was a pilot. There was also Mrs Tlang Sam Ell with her three teenage boys varying in age from thirteen, eighteen, and twenty. Mrs Tlang Sam Ell's husband was a high-ranking soldier. Then there was Mrs Chhor Vy who had two daughters, a son and a twenty-five-year-old sister named Reth.

These families had adults who could work together to build a shelter together. My family had nobody to turn to for help and we did not even have any tools or skills to make a watertight shelter or any kind of bed that would enable us to sleep off the ground. We had to use four small sticks to support a grass and leaf roof which only gave us shade but was utterly useless in a heavy rainstorm. For several days, worms and caterpillars dropped on us from the roof consisting of leaves. We all hated these crawling creatures and were terrified of them. But what else could we do?

9

A few days later the Khmer Rouge called us for a meeting. We were sitting in a group with ten other families.

They picked Mrs Chhor Vy to be the chief of the family group. Then, they selected a person to become Mekang, head of the group, who would be in charge of the ten families. My mother and the rest of the women had to go to the fields to collect straw for grass panels which were used as roof of a shelter. For my mother to go out into the fields, she had to leave my little sister with my grandmother.

Unlike Communism elsewhere, the Khmer Rouge praised rural peasantry, communal living, and farming. The ultimate goal was to become self-reliant through agricultural collectivism.

Every morning all the women, about five or six of them, were ordered out into the fields to collect grass, and every day, mother returned carrying a big bunch of grass on top of her head, with cuts all over her fingers and hands. If any of the women did not go to collect grass Mrs Chhor Vy would denounce them to the Khmer Rouge guards. She would tell them that the absentee was lazy and deserved to lose some of the food allowances.

In due course, Mrs Chhor Vy became conceited with her appointed title. She was tall, fair-skinned, thin, and liked to talk behind people's back. She enjoyed ordering people about and reporting to the head of Angkar anybody she did not like.

Mrs Chhor Vy criticised my mother and told Angkar that she did not collect the grass fast enough and that she could drive a car. The comment about being able to drive a car put us in danger. If Angkar believed that she could drive, she would be considered a 'rich capitalist', and often people disappeared for crimes like that.

How spiteful Mrs Chhor Vy became. Mother knew her from Phnom Penh as she was my uncle's neighbour. She had an odd character and acted flirtatiously towards the Khmer Rouge. It was her way of keeping herself safe.

Mrs Chhor Vy's children were so hungry, that they picked up earthworms to eat. I saw that with my own eyes. They washed them with ashes, stuck the worms on sticks and grilled them on the log fire. When I looked at their faces, they were more like skeletons. They had lost their hair and their swollen faces were covered with thin parchments of yellow waxy skin. Mrs Chhor Vy was too busy informing on people and left her children to their own devices while she went to collect grass with the group. This did not happen with others. Mrs Yim Pan Yee's children did not eat any of that, because they were supervised by their mother all the time.

We carried on living and trying to survive but the Khmer Rouge set aside a measly daily allowance for us. One cup of rice for my mother and myself, but only half a cup for my brothers, sister, and grandmother, because they did not work.

We received our allowance once a week. The rice allowance was sometimes mixed with corn and sometimes with a strange kind of wheat that we had never eaten before. We had to boil the wheat for a very long time or soak it overnight to make it edible. Searching the forest floor sometimes we sometimes found leaves, plants, or mushrooms that could be mixed in with the rice to make it more bearable. There were mushrooms that grew in the forest, but unfortunately, I did not know which ones were safe to eat. They looked delicious, so I picked them and took them home and showed them to others to find out if they were poisonous or not. Someone warned us not to eat them just in case they were poisonous. We needed food so my mum cooked them. What choice did she have? Afterwards, we were all very sick and felt ill but fortunately, we survived as the poison was mild.

The days when we found edible leaves, or a few edible mushrooms, were our lucky days.

Five of us lived in a little hut on a small piece of land given to us by Angkar. It was hard work to make the ground even and to build a hut. The ground was pretty uneven and had a huge dead tree trunk in the middle of it. Wrapped around the trunk was a huge mound, constructed by termites. The hut was raised about a meter off the ground and was so small that you could only take two large paces each way. Other men from the group helped us to build our hut.

My mum and I went to collect grass every morning though we did not have any proper cutting equipment. There was no time to dry the grass, so we would just weave it around some sticks to construct a thatched roof and walls. There were no nails or wires to build the hut, so instead, we used climbing plants and vines which we collected from the forest to tie things in place. Our beds were made from small branches, which was very uncomfortable. I slept next to my grandmother, whilst Sokbonn and Kosal slept alongside my mother and my sister.

It was a blessing that we had kept two mosquito nets. Without these nets, our whole family would have succumbed to sickness far quicker than we did. Many people of the ten families in our camp soon started to suffer from malaria. Between us we had a few quinine tablets left, but these were not enough to protect us. When my brother, Kosal, and I contracted malaria, my mum divided each of the tablets into quarters and gave them to Kosal and me. It helped for a few days.

Malaria had its own routine. I began to realise that it would start every day at midday and expected its invasive effects around noon. At first, I felt very cold and would shiver uncontrollably, which was followed by sweating, a feverish temperature, and a massive headache. We took turns to help each other when it started. My mother put some rocks by the fire and wrapped them up in any thick clothes that she could find. The hot rocks helped us to keep warm. When I was shaking, my brothers would sit on top of me to try to ease things, but no matter how many people sat by me, I still felt cold. After a long while I started to feel tired and sleepy, my head throbbed – I was sweating and was sick. Then, the sickness would go as quickly as it came. But the temporary relief did not mean that I was cured.

Malaria affected people differently. For some it discoloured their skin, while for others their body, arms, legs, and faces would swell up. That is how the disease took effect on my sister, Bonnary. Her face swelled up like a water balloon, so much that I often thought that if we were to prick her swollen skin, water might come out. The malaria repeatedly attacked all of us. We had to constantly endure malnutrition and disease.

Mrs Chhor Vy's daughters and sister died from malaria and Mrs Yim Pan Yee's family died one by one. All her children were beautiful, sweet, and well brought up. Soon after, Mrs Yim Pan Yee died too. Their family had dollars but did not have any gold or diamonds to exchange for the scraps of food that would have helped to keep them alive.

The rice that Angkar provided every comrade was not enough to keep anyone alive. Death quickly came to those who only relied on the rations that they were given.

The local villagers realised that the people from the city would need help to survive and some of them smuggled food to us in the forest.

Their help did not come for free but, at the time, food was more important than gold or diamonds. My mother had to exchange the jewellery that she had kept hidden ever since we left Phnom Penh for the food that the villagers smuggled past the Khmer Rouge guards. The villagers appeared with their goods hidden discreetly under their baskets; a tin of palm sugar, salt, dry salted fish, or more rice could prolong our life a little longer.

My mum did not care how valuable her jewellery was, how hard she had worked for it, or how long she had saved up to buy it – she just wanted us to be alive and well. If they discovered the food, we would be executed. If the guards had discovered the exchange, we all would have been punished or led to execution but fortunately, they never found out.

Although we were surrounded by people, being in the jungle felt lonely. Even the illusion that we would one day return to Phnom Penh no longer kept us company. We were stranded in the jungle with strangers from different families. But this unknown place and these unknown people were our home now.

Angkar had spies in the family camp who would listen to us at night and report any conversations that were considered anti-regime. My mum's stories about life before had to stop and we no longer dared to talk about our life in Phnom Penh. We could not even whisper to each other about our memories – too many people had disappeared after they had been overheard. This was especially difficult as we could not even take comfort in telling stories of the old days, when we were happy and together.

Mrs Tor, *tor* meaning 'lion', was the head of the family group. She knew us from Phnom Penh: her husband was a colonel in the army at the same base as my stepfather. Our acquaintance meant that our lives could be in danger if she informed on us. When her husband got killed before Phnom Penh fell to the Khmer Rouge, she visited our house for comfort and help. Mother gave money to help her and her young children, and now Mrs Tor stayed loyal to us. She told my mother how to be safe from Angkar's spies: we had to stop talking or behaving like we were from Phnom Penh. Instead, we had to make ourselves appear like peasants. The villagers who smuggled in food arranged the exchanges through Mrs Tor, who arranged for us to be a part of the trade.

10

The jungle area where we were living was close to the Thai border. Some people talked discreetly about escaping across the Thai border, but for us there was no way to escape. Others said that no one could survive. If you were not caught by the Khmer Rouge or the minefields, the jungle would surely get you killed.

Finally, after many weeks and months in the jungle, we were told the name of the area. It was called Chambok Thom in Korng Keurt forest. All of those who were sent there, were made up of those from Phnom Penh city and a couple of other provinces. We did not make friends and did not want to get to know anyone, to keep ourselves safe.

Life was getting harder. Sometimes we were given corn instead of rice. Cambodia had produced plenty of rice and export to sell in neighbouring countries like Thailand and Vietnam, and I wondered why they still did not have enough rice to feed us. Hunger and starvation were new to us. We fed pigs corn, rice dust, and vegetables, but we had never experienced surviving on it ourselves. The only thing we ate was fresh corn on the cob. In these conditions and with nothing else, the corn tasted delicious and softened our malaise.

It was strange not to find any birds in the jungle but here, there was no birdsong. However, at night we could hear crickets, frogs, and wild animals howl like wolves and when it was raining, we often heard the bullfrogs calling to each other. Some people went hunting at night and the next morning, we saw that some people were cooking frogs, bullfrogs, toads, and crickets for their dinner. Some of the people died from it. I did not know at the time, but certain toad's skins are poisonous.

Grandmother was getting weaker and could not walk or do things for herself. We had to give her baths, change her clothes, and look after her. With the help of Mrs Tor, my mother exchanged her jewellery for chicken, eggs, and rice from the villagers' black market. The exchange between smugglers and us had to be discreet and fast as it would have been dangerous if we were caught. We were very excited to have properly cooked rice with boiled eggs.

One afternoon while my grandmother was asleep, my mum quietly cooked the rice and eggs so we could have enough to share among us. Grandmother woke up, asking, "What are you doing?" We refused to lie to her, so we had to share some rice with my grandmother. I took two or three spoons of rice and an egg to feed her, lifting her head up to put the food in her mouth, but she was not able to swallow. I kept asking her to eat more but she simply could not. Soon my grandmother was so weak that she could not get up. She did not moan, groan, or complain that she had any pain or illness, she just felt weak.

It was December, it was cold and the temperature dropped in the jungle so we put rocks on the campfire to make it warm, then wrapped them up with old clothes to use as hot water bottles. We kept the fire burning all day and night.

Grandmother had diarrhoea too, we cleaned her, and changed her into her best clothes that she brought with her, a silk skirt, and a white blouse. She wanted us to exchange them for food, but we would not let her, we respected her and wanted her to be in the cleanest clothes possible.

At midday, I tried to feed grandmother rice and boiled egg, but she still was not able to swallow anything. She was quiet with her eyes closed and did not talk at all – she must have been too tired. That night was cold with a strong wind, so we all gathered close together under one large mosquito net. I slept next to my grandmother. Next to her was Sokbonn, Kosal, and my sister slept next to my mum, at the end of the row. It was a very dark, cold, quiet night, but we could hear the strong wind blowing against our hut.

During the night, my grandmother called out my nickname loudly in a clear voice, "Neang! You must be alert, run fast if anything happens, be careful, son." All the others heard her voice too, but we were too tired and cold to wake or respond and we kept ourselves wrapped up in blankets. I could not sleep because it was so cold. Later, I heard the cockerels crow, meaning that it must have been nearly 4 or 5 am. I saw a little blue light float out into the air up the ceiling of the roof and thought to myself that it must have been a glow worm or something. Then, I turned to check my grandmother as she slept next to me.

I touched her hand. It was cold. In shock, I woke my mum and told her that my grandmother had died.

My mother cried, but I could not. I felt sad and quiet, yet relieved that grandma had gone. At least, she was no longer in pain or suffering. At sunrise, in the morning, other people from our group heard the news and they came to see us, and some people brought rice for the funeral. The Khmer Rouge came to tell us that it was unnecessary to cry.

Many years later, I found a note from my mother's diary, marking the day of grandmother's death. It simply said: "Mother, *Om Sagneam*, passed away in the jungle *Cham Bok Thom* on Saturday night the 29th of December 1975."

The next morning, we arranged for my grandmother's funeral. A few men from the group came to help us prepare. Some went to find wood while others dug the hole in the ground. The crematorium was a few meters away from our hut. We wrapped grandmother's body in the best sleeping mat we had, even though we needed it to sleep on.

The men carried her body out of the hut, and we followed them to the hole that they had dug. They laid her body on a pile of wood and we stood there in silence and prayed. We were lucky to have someone who could conduct the funeral ceremony for us. He was young, but he knew the Buddhism chanting. Then they set fire to the wood.

I watched the ceremony from the start without words, then sat down and cried like I had never cried before. My mother, brothers, and sister left the place, but I stayed to watch the fire, eating her. I was in pain and could not believe what was going on in front of me.

Life is so cruel that she had her funeral that way. One time in Phnom Penh, my grandmother fell very ill. My mother thought that she would not survive, so, just in case, she prepared a funeral for my grandmother. She bought pieces of the best mahogany wood ready to make a coffin for grandmother which she stored in an empty room in our house in Phnom Penh.

Now, she had to be cremated without a proper funeral, no coffin, just on a pile of wood in the jungle. Nothing is permanent in this world. I did not cry at my father's funeral but now I was devastated.

After a while, I left the cremation and headed to the hut where my mum was busy preparing food for the people who helped us. Even though we did not have enough food to eat, it was our custom to thank people for their help.

The following morning, my mum and I collected my grandmother's bones from the ashes. We washed and carefully wrapped them with a piece of white cloth. She made a little pouch to keep my grandmother's bones and always kept it with her unless she had to go to work in the fields.

My mother was now the head of the family. She was a strong mother. We had seen many people lose their strength, just give up and die, but my mum had the strength – or at least never showed us any weakness. She told me many years later that there were many times at nights, when she could not sleep, she would lie awake and stare at us, her children, accompanied by her worries. If she died or committed suicide, we would have become orphans. Without her, what would the children's future be? With these thoughts in mind, she felt that she had to be strong and carry on living for her children's sake.

Grandmother Om Sagneam

11

We lost track of time, days, and months and we continued living in fear and without hope. Often, we looked to the sky and prayed for anyone out there to come to rescue us from our torment. We judged the time by how far our chilli seeds had grown. Of course, Angkar told us that what we had grown belonged to them and that we were not allowed to pick anything for ourselves.

The Khmer Rouge ordered everyone in the group to give up their valuable possessions to Angkar. They appointed an old couple in charge of collecting them from our group. The husband's name was Phaov, but I cannot remember his wife's name. Mother gave her a gold bangle to prove this was all we had left. It was like we were being mugged of our last scraps.

Again, we were interrogated by Khmer Rouge soldiers. What did we do when General Lon Nol's regime was in charge in Phnom Penh? As Mrs Tor had taught us, we pretended to be peasants, even though we knew that they would not believe us. I told them that I was a newspaper boy, that I delivered papers on the street. My mother said that she was a servant, a housekeeper for an upper-class family, and my father had been a chauffeur. Fortunately, we had lost all our documents and so there was nothing to prove otherwise, and nothing that the Khmer Rouge could trace.

Our hunger eroded any remaining hope; our family's rice allowance was often late and sometimes there was no rice at all. Only our tears could soften whatever scraps we had. We shared a small bowl each. Our hunger made it taste good, until the stomach cramps and diarrhoea came.

Waves of malaria engulfed me as often as the coming of tides. It would start in my spine; I would feel cold and start to shake. I wouldn't be able to stand, so would lie down. My mum would cover me with all the blankets we had and the hot stones from the campfire. After an hour, I would start to sweat, and my head would throb terribly. If mother had a fragment of quinine left, she would give it to me. Soon, my skin and eyes were the colour of dying leaves.

They called the adults, the head of each family from the whole village for a meeting one evening a week. As we sat in rows of ten, the Khmer Rouge lectured us about Angkar and how good it was that they had rescued us from capitalism under the Americans. Then they called for volunteers to tell them who was lazy in the fields, to denounce others who were not working hard enough, and who was weak and slow. They wanted us to criticise each other and inform on them. I sat in silence with a blanket wrapped over my head to protect me from mosquito bites as well as the Khmer Rouge's poisonous words. It was a cold dark night with stars shining from the sky.

Soon families were divided into groups: adults, teenagers, and young children. I was sent out every morning with the group of teenagers to collect grass or cut trees following the Angkar orders. It was decreed that everyone must be happy to work in the jungle; there would be no moaning or resting. When we saw the black uniforms, we hated them. We hated their red scarves and their black caps. Some of them kept showing off their watches and showed each other what they had. I did not dare to look them directly in the eye. Head down – we had to stay anonymous.

One night, Mrs Tor called me to join a meeting. It seemed that there were only teenage boys at the meeting. Mrs Tlang Sam Ol's three teenage sons, who lived in the hut opposite ours, were there too. We sat in rows of ten. From the light of the moon, I could see the silhouette of the Khmer Rouge soldier that stood in front of us. Mrs Tor sat next to me. The soldiers repeated their usual mantras and propaganda. Capitalism: bad. Khmer Rouge: good. America: bad.

Then they broke the news that Angkar needed to select teenagers from our village to go and study. They called out names from the list, one by one until my name was called. I answered excitedly and stepped forward. I thought that I had been selected to go back to school, to my books and to my home in Phnom Penh. Suddenly, I heard Mrs Tor loudly say that it was not my name called. I was Sokphal Din and not Sokphal. She told me to sit down back in the row. I did. The Khmer Rouge soldier did not argue, and they continued to call other names. After they finished with their list, we were told to sit separately from those who were going to be educated. Two of Mrs Tlang Sam Ell's sons were in that group. I never saw them again after that night.

The Khmer Rouge then went on telling us about how strong they were; they claimed victory and bragged about how they had destroyed capitalism. It went on and on. We must obey Angkar and work hard for Angkar. Near midnight, we could go back home to sleep.

Swollen legs, arms, bellies, and faces. Diarrhoea. Shivering. Sweating. Cuts that would not heal and spread deep to the bone were followed by maggots. This became a daily routine.

Since we had been on the train, I had not seen my cousin, You Sotta, or as we called him, Nhok, the third son of my Uncle Mr You Ol. So, we were shocked to see him arrive at our hut in the jungle. We thought that his mother sent him to find us, but he told us that he was escaping and planned to cross the Thai border. It was an impossible journey, but his mother had given him some valuable things, so he could use them along the way for whatever he needed. People gossiped about those who had tried to escape across to the Thai border. Some got caught, killed, lost, or blown up by the land mines that had been planted.

Nhok ate dinner and stayed overnight with us. We did not ask him when he would leave or what route he would take. The less we knew, the better.

The next morning, before any of us woke up, he had departed on his treacherous journey. I realised that he had taken the only pair of shoes that I had left. They were not special shoes or anything, just plastic flip flops, but they were my most valuable possession at the time. So precious that they could have even been exchanged for gold or diamonds.

The jungle took Nhok, just like it took my cousins, aunts, and uncles, and that was the last time we ever saw him.

A few weeks, or maybe months later, my mother suddenly thought about one of our relatives. We had been separated from the rest of our family at a train station and in thinking back, it seemed that there were only oxcarts waiting for us, not for them. Then we were told to get on any oxcart or buffalo cart as quickly as possible. We were so tired and did not have the energy to find anyone at that moment. We just wanted to get to the destination quickly, so we could rest and had been separated.

We knew about our relative's location from You Sotta, who had recently found us. Apparently, they were scattered around to settle in the jungle and the Khmer Rouge had created small villages made up of families from Phnom Penh. We were living in Cham bok Thom village, whilst my aunt and her children were living in another village. Aunt Horm Sopheoun was living nearby, but unfortunately, my Aunt Sokhom with her three children were living in a different area in the jungle.

One day, my mother went on to request permission from the head of the village group to find and visit them. Luckily, they allowed us a day visit to my aunt's village. We did not even know the exact location or distance. We left brother and sister at the hut and we went off towards their village. We started in the early morning walking through bushes, trees, under an unbearably hot sun shining on our head.

At midday, we found the village. I could not remember how we knew the way to find the village. Their village looked exactly like our village. They were all built from tree branches, bamboo with grass roofs. It was very quiet midday, when we found my mother's sister-in-law Mrs Horm Sophin's hut (You Sotta's mother). We went straight into the hut to find her lying flat on a bamboo bed. She was very ill, with her body, arms, and face swollen and pale, yellow skin. She could not move or get up to greet us except by we knew she was happy from the tears in her eyes. We asked her about the rest of her family who came with her. It appeared that most of them had died of malaria and she too was suffering with the disease. We were very sad to hear about it. We told her that her son has been at our hut. She said that she gave him lots of valuable pieces of jewellery for his journey to help him to escape from the jungle. She looked tired and I knew that she was dying. Without food and medicine, and with malaria, we would all die.

I saw one of my other cousins, You Sokha (Aunt Horm Sophin's fourth son), but we hardly said anything to each other. I just asked him about other relatives, to which he responded with heart-breaking answers. I did not see my cousin You Sam Eourn, who was three years my senior. He was born in the year of the horse. We were best friends and went to the same college in Phnom Penh. I felt sad because he was the cousin that had only just started speaking to me again after a falling out over me getting my diploma.

I was tired, upset, hot, and hungry, and did not want to know all the sad news. We were talking with my aunt for a short while, but we had to leave, heading back home before sunset. I do not think that we had anything to eat at her place. That was the last time that I saw my aunt and her son, You Sokha. They all died afterwards.

At the same time, we saw other two cousins Nort and Chan who were with us in Chanlok village. Her family lived next to my Aunt Sophin's hut. We did not go to their hut as they told us that all the old women relatives had died, including her mother Mrs Horm Sopheoun. This was only one or two months after we were separated in the jungle. We lost many relatives in a very short period of time.

I did not know how my mum felt about seeing my aunt and I did not ask. We just walked back through the jungle quietly.

A few months after we left Phnom Penh, we lost many of our relatives at the hands of the Khmer Rouge. Who would be next? It could be any of us.

We came back to our hut at Cham Bok Thom village carrying sadness and great disappointment in our hearts.

I could not avoid selection forever. One day, I was summoned by the village chief and told to join the group of young male teenagers who were being sent to a labour camp. When the time of our departure arrived, mother prepared some roasted rice flakes, called Ambok, to take with me.

I joined the group of teenagers from the village and walked with them through the forest all day until dusk. When the Khmer Rouge decided that we should stop, the group scrambled around to find a flat area to sleep. The ground was uneven, hard, and rough. I ate the rice flakes that mother had prepared for me and laid out my mat.

I was surprised to see that my cousin, You Sam Euorn or Ngoy, had also been selected and was laying out his mat too. He had been sent to the labour camp from his family group and I was very pleased to see him and tried to make conversation, asking how he was. He did not say much but I could see that he looked pale, thin, and sad. Neither of us made much more conversation, we were tired, hungry, and it was getting dark.

I remember my friendship with Sam Euron back in Phnom Penh. Whenever he had money, he took me out to the cinema or a fruit shake after college. He asked me if I had any food that he could have. In the beginning, I lied, but then I felt bad and decided to give him some rice flakes. I could not remember if we slept next to each other or not but when I woke up the next morning, he had gone off with another group. That was the last time that I saw him.

It became usual for our group to move around from place to place. We would work and then move on, going wherever the Communists needed us. Over time, I was sent to many hard-labour camps and joined in many different groups of teenagers. Some groups were better than others. I was weak and thin and was not as strong as some of the others. However much I denied my past to the Khmer Rouge, all the workers could see that I was from Phnom Penh and that I had never worked in the fields before.

One time, I was sent with a group of twenty workers. The head of the group was local to the area. He was about two years older than the rest of us and spoke with a different accent. He had the power to punish us or inform on us to the Khmer Rouge guards if we did not obey his orders. After we had walked all day till late into the afternoon, we stopped by a stream to set up a camp and eat. When the communal rice was ready, we sat in groups of ten and received our food allowance.

The head of the group seemed to take a special interest in me. He jokingly told the rest of the group to leave me alone as I was going to be his 'personal assistant'. I had to arrange my sleeping area close to him and I obeyed, setting up my mat just a few meters away from him. Then that night I heard him call my name to come to his place. "Comrade Neang, come over here, I have a fever, I need your help."

I crawled to him in the dark. He told me to get in his mosquito net with him to help. He lay on the ground and he asked me to sit next to him and in a trembling voice asked me to put my hand on his body to feel his temperature. He took my hand and moved it over his body. I was innocent. The next morning, we started to move again. Nothing was said. The group was split up as it always was. Later, I was told that the head of the group had died.

12

Weeks and months went by without knowing how long we spent in the Kong Keourt jungle. Starvation and illness followed our every move. If we had any illnesses, we had to scavenge for herbal plants and try to cure ourselves. The Khmer Rouge sought out those who were ill and sent them to the 'hospital'. None of them returned.

This was not the last time that I was selected to go to a youth labour camp. Another time, after an exhausting walk over sharp bamboo stems and hot sand, we arrived at the camp and they told us to sit in a row of ten for a roll call of names. A leader was then appointed to each group. My group leader was the son of a peasant farmer from a village nearby. He had a strong accent and was short and muscular. We called him 'brother' or 'comrade Pub'. They gave us a bowl of cooked rice and a few grains of salt to eat and then they showed us our bamboo shelters, which we needed to share with four others.

At dawn, we were given a cup of rice soup with salt. We stood in line and sat with the group in a circle on the ground to eat. They cooked the rice soup in a giant metal wok or oil barrel. The 'chef' did not stir the rice evenly, so some people had to endure the rice juice with hardly any rice grain in it while others were lucky enough to have a thicker rice porridge. Whatever filled our bowl simply reminded us of how hungry we were and how weak we had become. But in labour camps, weakness was not an option. Not working was not an option. And those who did not work had their food allowance cut, only getting a cup of rice soup at midday. If any were ill too often the Khmer Rouge threatened with sending them to the so-called hospital. We all knew what that meant.

Every one of us, boys, girls, men, and women, was given a hoe and a pair of baskets made from bamboo to carry soil. Along with the hoe and baskets came a target, a certain number of meters that had to be dug.

Sometimes, I was given a sickle for harvesting rice. Rain or shine, we planted rice. Leeches were our constant companion, sticking to our legs and sucking our blood. The first time the leeches journeyed up my ankles to my knees, I betrayed the secret of my background. In panic and fear, I ran out of the paddy field to higher ground. At the time, I did not even care if the Khmer Rouge guards punished me. I quickly learned to tie my trouser legs up to stop leeches crawling up.

Working from dawn to midday. A bowl of rice. Working again until 6 pm. Rice for dinner. After dinner, a meeting to tell us that we needed to work faster, and how city people were lazy. The rows of ten people at the meetings were different each time. Gaps appeared and faces disappeared. Quiet selections took the weaker workers away for execution.

One very dark cool night, I heard someone scream in pain. It was Phan Naroth, or Vanna, a cook from the camp kitchen, who had been caught stealing. He was being tortured and begged for mercy. The four of us in our hut kept quiet and tried to sleep. I did not see Vanna in the kitchen the next day and we did not ask anyone about it.

Every workday was supervised by the Khmer Rouge 'comrades' armed with their Kalashnikov rifles. Any perceived display of weakness or laziness would be fatal. When I was not racing to plant rice and trying to avoid the leeches, I was sent to maintain the dykes in the paddy fields. We had to repair them, and seal the walls with mud so that the fields kept enough water.

Sometimes, we were sent to work on the watermills. The watermills were used to extract water from the stream and transfer it to the rice fields or take water out of the rice paddy if the level was too high. The mills were built with bamboo and ropes, and some of them had big wheels with spokes attached and were lifted high off the ground. It took two people pushing the wheels to bring water up and transfer it into the rice fields. I paddled the wheel with another person. We could not stop since we were constantly being watched.

13

I gambled one morning and pretended I was ill. I said that I had diarrhoea and fever and I could not muster the strength to work in the fields. The leader of the group sent me to see the 'Pol Pot doctor'. As it turned out, he was a teenage boy without any medical qualifications. I was instructed to go to the hospital, about ten kilometres from the hard-labour camp, so I packed my belongings and walked to the hospital.

I had never known anyone return from going to the hospital, but I wagered that I could find a chance to escape. I walked from morning till evening, but we were escorted by Khmer Rouge guards all the way, escape was impossible. From everything that I had heard about hospitals, I was sure that I was on my way to execution, but with unwavering hard labour as my alternative, it was a chance that I was willing to take. The hospital was a temple that the Khmer Rouge had appropriated, expelling the monks who had originally inhabited it. It was telling that the Khmer Rouge used sacred, holy ground to murder.

The guard left us with the doctor to check in to the hospital. There was no immediate execution. They asked my name and registered us in the main shrine room that the monks had used for special ceremonies. I could see that some of the Buddha statues had been destroyed or defaced; some were without heads. After I was registered, I went in to find a spot to lay my mat. No treatment or medicine was offered except their homemade herbal tablets that were round shaped like rabbit droppings. They had a sort of serum in bottles to inject which created abscesses. It was like they used us as guinea pigs, to experiment on.

We were given a cup of liquid rice twice a day. I scavenged for anything that I could mix with the rice to make soup that could perhaps fill my stomach a little more. I managed to find some water hyacinths from the pond next to the kitchen. And indeed, for ten minutes I felt better. Full. But then the liquid rice was expelled by my bowels. I was getting weaker and weaker.

After a few days at the hospital, I fell into hushed conversation with two older men. We talked guardedly about our background, and I found out that they were well-educated from Phnom Penh. It was a risk; they could have been informers that Angkar would often sneak into our groups to gain our trust and discover those who were disloyal. I told them about my plan to go back to my family at the village in the jungle. They advised me to write a fake note and show it to the head of the group at the village where my family lived. One of the men handed me a piece of paper and a fountain pen. It was an expensive Parker pen with a gold cap. Even the possession of such a pen betrayed his background and put him, and now me, in danger. I asked him to write the note for me as it could be risky if it was matched to my handwriting. One quiet afternoon while no one was around the three of us sat down to write the note. He wrote a few lines: *"Comrade Sokphal has been treated in Phnom Srok hospital. He can return back to stay at the village due to his slow recovery."*

I did not think about the consequences of being discovered. The two gentlemen told me to make myself look strong and appear ready to go back to work in the fields. The next morning, I woke up early, got myself ready and went to ask the doctor in charge for permission to leave the hospital. Permission was refused. I tried again the next day and was again refused permission. At daybreak on the third morning, I went straight to them apparently strong with a forced smile on my face. They let me leave that morning.

After I had my food allowance, I left the hospital with the note hidden in my pocket. The sun was not too hot to make my journey on my bare feet. So, I walked straight out of the hospital entrance and turned in the direction of the camp. The main road was covered in red gravel that snaked on for miles without any houses alongside it.

As soon as I was out of sight of the hospital, I turned off the road to the east. I supposed that the jungle must have been in that direction, so I walked on the bank of a rice paddy and followed the sun and used my shadow as a compass. Whenever I saw any groups of workers in the rice fields, I walked quietly with my head bowed. I prayed to get there safely and luckily, no one stopped me or asked any questions.

It was not an easy journey on the bank, the sides of the paddy fields were uneven, unsteady, and slippery. I fell down a few times into the muddy water but each time, I hauled myself back onto the bank with hope of seeing my family again. I did not stop walking until I reached the edge of the forest which I entered and followed the tracks on the ground. I kept walking deeper into the jungle to the east and just as I was losing hope, I saw some houses with straw roofs appear at a distance in front of me. That gave me energy and I walked on. At long last, I reached the village and went straight to find my family's hut.

My mother and I did not say much to each other when I arrived back at our hut. I told her about the note, and she took me to see the head of the group in the village. He did not query it and just told me to register for the rice allowance. As I was supposed to be ill, I was not allowed to work, meaning that my rice allowance was just two tins of rice grains per week. We returned to our routine of foraging any vegetation or edible foliage to mix with the rice to fill the pot. Even that was not enough.

14

Every morning my mother would leave with a group of women to harvest long grass which was used for roofing. She had to let the grass dry in the sun and braided the sharp blades into sheets, slicing her fingers. The village used the sheets to thatch roofs wherever the old ones became old and broken. She would leave my three-year-old sister with my younger brother Kosal alone in the house while she worked. We never laughed or smiled, nor did we talk about our past in Phnom Penh. It was a question of holding hope in our minds, afraid of losing it altogether.

The family group had grown smaller since I had been in the village as all the men were sent to work in the labour camps. They were permitted to come home to see their family for a day or two every couple of months. Fewer men returned each time.

After a while staying with my mother and family, I found it hard to cope with the sparse food allowance, and soon, we were starving. Sokbonn and Kosal were malnourished and had skinny bodies with swollen legs, we all had malaria and diarrhoea. We had to take turns looking after each other when malaria struck. The blankets were prepared, and the stones put in the fire. When it was my turn, I would wrap myself in the blankets and lie down, shaking. My sister and both brothers would sit on top of me to help control my trembling. Mother would then wrap the heated stones we prepared and placed them next to my body. After the attack had passed, I would sleep for many hours, as was the case for my mother and brothers.

Luckily, my sister did not suffer from malaria badly, but she suffered from horrible stomach pain and constant diarrhoea. Her whole body, arms, legs, and face were swollen. Every time I came back from the labour camp, it seemed to have gotten worse.

I decided to go back to the youth labour camp at Kork Rom Chek as my family could not survive if they kept having to share their food allowance with me and I knew that I would not live if I stayed. At least at the camp, I would get a rice bowl, twice a day. Hunger made it so that I needed the camp more and I needed my family in order to survive.

I left my family in the late morning, saying goodbye to my brothers and sister with tears in my eyes, not looking back. With no real knowledge of the location of the labour camp, I walked directionless in the rain. When I arrived at the camp at sunset, it was dark, quiet, and wet. There was no one there to register me and the only dry place that I could find was the cattle stable filled with ox and buffalo. It smelt terrible and was infested with insects and mosquitos but I had no choice other than to find a space next to an ox and lay my mat down. About midnight the ox defecated over my head, but I was too tired to move.

The next morning, I introduced myself to the chief of the group who did not ask any questions and assigned me a workgroup again. I was given two tins of rice grain and a half tablespoon of salt each day. I did not use all the rice allowance, I saved some of it every day, hoarding it for later to give to my family.

Every day from sunrise to dusk was the same routine, without a weekend or holiday: planting rice, patching damaged dikes, and working on the water wheel to water the rice paddy.

Water wheel (Photo credit DC-CAM)

When the harvest season came, I was given a plot of land to work with as well as an assortment of others. We had to complete our targets otherwise we were not allowed to leave the field, even if it meant staying through the night. The Khmer Rouge guards checked every hut for absentees. They had their own kind of regime: they lectured, they ate, they talked, they teased, they laughed, and they flirted with each other. I hated them and their easy lives. To distract myself, I focused on food: every grain of rice. Each one was precious, and each one that fell to the ground, I picked up. Some people caught insects, crickets, snakes, crabs, fishes, little frogs, or anything they could eat while they were working in the rice fields. They kept them in their pockets or wrapped it in their scarfs to eat later. Some of them caught some shrimp while working, they ate them raw, there and then. I chewed raw rice grains while I harvested, just to suck the juice out of them, praying that it would help to appease my growling stomach.

One day, my brother Sokbonn arrived at the camp, with him he had a note from my mother. She wrote asking me to come home to see my younger brother Kosal, who was ill with malaria. I could not believe how Sokbonn could walk that far from the jungle, just to find me at the campsite. I went to ask the head of my group if I could go home for a few days to see my ill brother. They asked me, "Why you need to see your brother? Are you a doctor? Are you going to make him better?"

After a few days of begging, he let me go to see my family for a few days. I went straight to my hut and packed some rice and dried fish that I saved for my mum.

Kosal had little hair left on his head but he kept a brave smile on his face. I felt so helpless that I did not know how to help my brother with his illness. I gave my mother all the rice grain, salt, some dried fish, and dried rats that I had saved from the camp. These were the luxury items that I had managed to obtain, and that night my brothers feasted on the rat's meat. We had dinner together in tears of joy.

The day of my departure came round quickly and when it did, Kosal begged me to stay. I explained to him that I had to go back, otherwise I would be in trouble. I walked away, again not daring to look back though I could hear my brother Kosal's crying voice. He screamed with trembling words, shouting, "Please brother don't leave us, don't go, please don't go. These evil people are taking my brother away from me. You will all burn in hell."

Even today I remember his words, his voice echoing in my head. But still, I walked away. My mum tried to comfort Kosal and pleaded with him not to cry. I got back to the camp in the dark and started to work again the next day.

A few days later, Mrs Tlang Samel's youngest son brought me a note. My brother Kosal had died.

My chest was cold and numb. I felt guilty that I had left him. Mother did not say much in the note about what happened or how he died. It was brief. Like Kosal's life. I asked the head of the group for permission to travel to my family, but he refused and I worked that day as usual.

A few weeks later, the rainy season came and the rice fields in Kouk Romcheck were underwater with no higher ground to go to. Angkar told us to leave the camp and go back to the villages to our families.

That night, I was kept up by my thoughts longing to be with my mother, brother, and sister at home, who were now without Kosal. I walked through the rice fields, across the mud trudging through deep water. After a few hours, I could see the shadow of the forest and trees where my family's village was, where the villagers were preparing to move to higher ground. The water flooded just a few metres away from our hut. Before we left, I wanted to say goodbye to Kosal and I asked my mother to show me his grave. She told me that it was at the edge of the forest which was now flooded, and the water had covered all the landmarks, so she could not remember exactly where it was. Kosal was a lovely brother and I loved him dearly.

The water destroyed all the plants and vegetables that we grew and used to improve our bland rations of rice. We dug out all the herbs, like chillies, basils, lemongrass that we could find to take with us and try to replant them on higher, drier ground.

That evening, I gave my mum rice from the food allowance that I had saved, and we had dinner together. It was nothing like the dinners that we used to have in Phnom Penh and the family was no longer complete now that we had lost Kosal.

Mother's hair was so short it looked almost shaven, yet it was still thicker and healthier than the rest of her thin body. My sister, Bonnary, was swollen and bloated, while Sokbonn's skin hung loosely over his bones. I was not sure what I looked like because we did not have access to a mirror and I am not sure that I wanted to know. We had nothing to clean ourselves with; no soap, nor toothpaste, and we only had a bowl of watery rice to eat and a shelter, that needed repair, as a home.

The road was now cut off with water and we had to move before everything was washed away. We hoisted our belongings onto our shoulders and on my mother's head. Sokbonn carried as much as he could in his small eight-year-old arms. The water was up to our waist, and the current was strong. We waded through, knowing that if we slipped, we would be carried away. Night fell but we kept moving. My mum would carry our belongings 10 or 15 meters before putting them down on any available higher ground and going back to carry my sister the same distance. She held my sister close to her chest until she had to leave her and go back to retrieve our belongings.

Each time this happened, my sister was scared and began screaming as she saw my mum walk away from her. She cried, "Mum please don't leave me, where are you? Please don't leave me."

We walked all night long until daylight, the rain lashing at our feet, pushing us off the track. When we walked in the water it was impossible to see where to place our feet: there were rocks and roots which made us cut our feet and fall. There was nothing to guide us – no one to help.

Finally, a huddle of people pointed us to some safe ground. It was decided that we would stop there for the night. Nothing was dry but at least it was away from the flow of the water. The next day, we realised that the huddle of people were villagers and when we spoke to them, they revealed that they came from a village called Poy Cha, next door to the settlement of Trapeang Tmor. They had not been forced to leave their homes like us because they were Angkar's people and were rice farmers, not city dwellers.

Angkar ordered them to let us stay in what had previously been their village.

All around us were signs of a real village, which was much nicer and more habitable than the collection of huts that we had known in the jungle. There were coconut trees, bananas, and many edible plants in gardens. We were ordered to stop in front of a large wooden house that had been built high off the ground on tall cement pillars. Five other families had been allocated the same house and it was decided that we could stay under the house, towards the back. Our area was sectioned off by four large wooden boards which were each just over one-metre square. There were more wooden boards, raised off the ground by four wooden blocks which we used to sleep and eat. When it rained, we had to sit up because the wind sprayed rainwater all over us.

At night, we listened to the bullfrogs and crickets and reminisced about the past.

Teacher Lang owned the house with his eldest son Thor Kimlon who was the head of the children group in the village and was proud to work for Angkar. Lang's wife, Eng, was friendly with us as she knew that we were from the city and that we had valuable possessions like diamonds and gold. My mother exchanged her diamond rings, pendant, bracelets with Eng for rice. All of Lang's family were healthy because they grew many vegetables around their house and so did not live off the meagre rations that we were used to.

One of the families who lived under the house with us had a son, named Sarorn. His family were kind to us, they gave us fish and small crabs that they had caught in the paddy fields. In exchange, we gave them some of the rice that we had swapped for gold.

Sarorn was tall and strong, and after getting to know him a bit, he revealed to me that he had a plan. He persuaded me to go with him to steal yams from the field behind the house. I agreed to go with him and even told my mum about our plan, who did not object. When Sarorn decided that the time had come, he gave me a big sack and told me to follow him. We snuck out the back of the house in the dark and made our way past the mango trees, bushes of bamboo, and the open ground that all the families used as toilets. Fifty metres further on were the yams and sweet potato fields. I could not see anything except Sarorn's shadow, we stopped several times along the way to look and listen for signs of others. Sarorn told me to stay close to him and open the bag ready to collect yams. Though it was pitch black, I could still hear him pulling yams out of the ground. Whilst he harvested, I collected the yams and shoved them in the bag. When it was full, we turned to head back.

We got home safely, and my mum was waiting under the mosquito net as we separated yams between us quietly. She hid them under our bed, quickly burying them. As our fire always burned, we were able to bake one of the yams under the hot ashes straightaway. We tore into it. That night we slept well, with full stomachs. In the morning, teacher Lang informed us that thieves had ravaged the yam farm. We kept quiet and consumed our stolen yams as quickly as we could.

Srey Mech's mother was another woman from under the house who my mother became acquainted with, but we never found out her real name. Mother exchanged some of her gold for a pillow that Srey Mech's mother had. It was the only time that I argued and moaned at her. Instead of saving the gold for food, she had wasted it on a pillow. She had been conned. While I was saying that my mother threw a woodblock at me, which hit my left elbow and cut my skin. The wound caused an infection and scar. I later realised that the pillow was the one and only luxury she allowed herself during that time and needed it for comfort and to sleep better. We never talked about the pillow again.

Whilst I was sent to work on the repair of another dyke in a nearby village, my mum was tasked to make fertiliser for the fields. She was forced to mix human excrement with clays, smearing it thinly on the ground for it to dry in the sun. Then it was pounded into small pieces and spread on the rice fields. To try and stay as clean as she could, she tried to touch faeces as little as possible. The head of the group scolded my mother, "Old woman Penh, use all your fingers and hands properly! Is it because you were in the feudalism regime, did you used to have servants?" My mum told me that she did not respond and continued working in silence.

Again, I was back at the hospital. I was very ill with a skin infection. The head of the labour camp did not care about my health and simply sent me back home to save the hospital's rice allowance.

I do not know what caused the infection, but my skin blistered and pus oozed out of the popped blisters. I had no choice but to lay on the hospital ground, in full view of people. My mother brought a pot of boiled liquid mixed with plants, suggested by the villagers, and came to the hospital every day to tend to my wounds, cleaning out the pus with her bare hands. It was incredibly painful, and it did not work. The next day, more pus came up.

One morning, after I received a food allowance from the hospital, I went home to see my mum, which was not too far from the hospital. Patients could go where they wanted so I went and sat under the house waiting for my mother. While I was sitting on the bamboo bed under the front of the house, I saw a group of Khmer Rouge teenagers walking past the house.

Amongst them, I spotted a woman carrying a bag with a red cross printed on it. My first thought was that she must have been a doctor or medic so I walked straight to her and asked her, "Comrade! Do you have any antibiotics or penicillin?"

I explained to her about my skin infection that would not heal, showing her my infected hands. She did not answer but reached in her shoulder bag and pulled out two almost-empty bottles which I assumed was penicillin. She was a bit hesitant to give them to me because there was not much left in the bottles, but I begged her to give them to me and after a while, she reluctantly complied.

Straightaway I opened the cap and poured a few drops of boiled water inside the bottle, shook it, and applied on my hands and in between my fingers. It worked and the blisters, pus, and itching all stopped and healed the next day. It had been a miracle that I crossed that medic, she must have been an angel who had come to bless me.

15

While I was away working at the youth labour camp my brother Sokbonn was caught stealing pumpkin leaves. He was eight years old and so thin that the blue veins running across his body were bigger than his muscles, and his ribs stuck out like a skeleton's. Hunger had made his hair fall out. Like all of us, to soothe his hunger Sokbonn scavenged for leaves to add to our rice pot, but unfortunately, he stumbled upon the wrong vegetable patch.

When he was walking along the edge of a field, he picked a few flowers and some leaves of the edible pumpkin plant. A man who had noticed Sokbonn picking the pumpkin leaves, suddenly grabbed him, tied his arms together and began to beat him. After Sokbonn cried and begged him to stop, the man dragged him over to a vicious red ant's nest and forced him to stand on it.

Fortunately, one of the villagers who saw what was happening, ran straight to my mother to tell her. She rushed to find Sokbonn, who was still tied up and standing on the red ant's nest. By now, Sokbonn's legs were covered by the biting red ants. The boy was crying, being tortured by the ants that were climbing towards his chest and face. Mother began to untie Sokbonn and started screaming at the man, "How could you do this? He is only a child, he was hungry, can't you see? He is thin and so hungry that he hardly has the energy to walk. How could you punish my son? Release him now."

The man was surprised at being challenged and scolded by my mother. He said to her, "How dare you talk to me that way old woman. Maybe it is because you used to live in Phnom Penh with your powerful husband from the capitalist army?"

The accusation could easily have led to my mother's execution, but she was not afraid and retorted, "Oh, you said that I am the wife of a lieutenant? How do you know that? Does that mean that you are working with my husband and working under him too? If I am called to stand in front of Angkar, I will tell them that you are a republic soldier too. You won't be safe either."

He did not say anymore and without another word, he let my mother further untie Sokbonn and take him home. She was so angry – she felt like she had been possessed by a demon to have the power to fight against the man like that. My brave mother was not afraid of him even if it meant facing death. She loved her children and to see anyone do that was unbearable.

During the pumpkin leaves' incident, I was working in the rice paddy close to our village. On the way back home from the rice fields, I was walking through vegetable plots and I noticed that there were cabbages planted along the way. It was nearly dark, so no one could see me, so I decided to pull up a few cabbages, and hide them under my scarf to take back home. I showed them to my mum and gave them to her. She was not happy and told me not to do that again as she was scared that, like Sokbonn, I would be caught. I replied that these cabbages did not belong to anyone, that even though Angkar claimed everything was theirs, they should have been available to all of us. I did not know what mother did with those cabbages, because I was so tired from my day in the paddies, so I let it go and went to bed. The next morning, I went off to work in the field as usual. When I returned that evening, my mother recounted a series of terrible events that had occurred while I had been at work.

Three Khmer Rouge soldiers with guns had been at our place – two women and a man. They had been told that some cabbages were stolen from the vegetable farm and we were the suspects. Without warning, they came up to our place searching us in broad daylight. It was a terrible shock, and everyone was terrified. It was a real possibility that we would be arrested or even taken for execution. Thankfully, the night before, my mother had hidden the cabbages in an old brown plastic suitcase that we found along the way from Phnom Penh. They searched around our sleeping area, through our clothes and even inside the suitcase. It was a miracle that they did not find the cabbages.

After they left, my mother went through the suitcase to find the cabbages. They were there, wilted, and dried. We were very lucky to escape death that day. I believed that my grandmother's spirit helped us. I never stole vegetables again.

Another time before this incident, we were searched inside out. Four Khmer Rouge guards came to search every family staying in the community house. Their target was to confiscate anything belonging that they wanted: plates, rice bowls, pots, and knives. They said that we did not need any of that anymore, because now we would be using the community canteen to eat meals together at the same time in the same place. They took many things from us on that day. To our horror, they found my mother's driving licence, on it was her picture and her details in Khmer and French. The soldiers could not read it and asked her about it to which she replied that the card was to identify her as a servant for the rich people.

They examined it but did not ask any further questions. They handed it back to my mother, and she let it fall on the floorboards. Mother slowly hid it under her feet and hoped they would forget about the card.

While they were searching, my mum was praying in her mind. Perhaps it was our lucky day. It was such a relief when they left, and she destroyed that card straight away, cutting it up and burning it.

After a few months of arriving in Poy Cha village, Angkar stopped giving rice as food allowance anymore. They built a large community canteen for people to either eat there or to take their food allowance home. Most people just took the cooked rice home, re-cooked it again, and added more vegetables. My mother had already exchanged all her jewellery for rice grain, corn, and dried fish with the villagers. Some of them had access to the rice stock or oversaw the canteen and never worked in the hard-labour fields like us. They were allowed to stay at home and look after their children. The woman who worked at the canteen managed to conceive a baby. Even though she suffered a miscarriage, she managed to get pregnant again. This showed that they were healthier than us and that they had access to plenty of nutrition, that we did not.

There was a time when my mum and I went to find my Aunt Sokhom, her sister-in-law. Two of my female cousins, Nout and Chan (Mrs Ham Sopheoun's daughters), were the last surviving members of their family.

It started when they happened to walk past my mother at Poy Cha village, which was such an unbelievable coincidence. They told us they had been sent to work hard-labour at the dyke construction site Trapeang Thmor.

Dam construction in hard-labour camp 1975 (Photo credit DC-CAM)

The last time I saw them was at the beginning of this tragedy when we were forced out of our home in Phnom Penh and walking along the road together. We were separated when we arrived at the jungle. Her father and two brothers were ordered to come forward and were taken away along with my father and another uncle You Sambath, also called Moth.

They told us where Aunt Sokhom was living and that the rest of their family had died. They had been sent to do hard-labour but were kept moving from camp to camp. It was a complete surprise and very fortunate that they met my mother by chance for the last time. We all cried when we heard the news. After that, we never saw or heard from them again.

However, that day they told my mother my Aunt Sokhom's whereabouts. They said that she lived in another village far away from us, but I cannot remember the name of that village. Aunt Sokhom had three children, a boy aged one, a girl aged five, and a boy aged seven. She lost two of her children and only seven-year-old Sokha was still alive. After my mother heard the news, she went to beg Angkar, requesting to have my aunt move from that village to stay with us in Poy Cha village. They gave us permission to take her back from that village and assigned us an oxcart and a driver to take us there. We left my sister and brother in Poy Cha and we headed off to get Aunt Sokhom.

It was a very hard journey, with bumpy roads through the forest and fields, but we did not stop. When we eventually got to her village, it was nearly sunset. We asked villagers and found Aunt Sokhom's son, Sokha. Sokha was overwhelmed, excited, and in tears at the same time and kept telling us about his mother. He said through his tears that we had come too late, and his mother was not well, she was not responding to him and was in a coma. We followed him to his hut where we found his mother laying on a bamboo bed. She could not move or talk; her eyes were half-closed and she was gasping for air. She must have heard, or perhaps she felt that we were there, because Sokha kept telling her of our presence. He said, "Mum, Mum, Om (aunt) and brother are coming to see us. They are coming to take us to live with them. We are going to live with them." I could see Aunt Sokhom with tears in her eyes. She must have heard but could not respond. We knew that she was not going to make it through the night, but we spent her last night in her village by her side. We never knew what happened from the day we lost each other and were separated on the journey to the jungle. My mother was sad, crying and very disappointed.

That night, I could not sleep, feeling very sad. How unfortunate it was that our lives were always so full of sadness. We had been excited to track her down and had envisioned her living with us in our village. I was sad to see her for the last time, in the last minutes of her life. Maybe it was her wish to have her son with us. We all said our last words, goodbye to her and wished her journey to a better place and we assured her that we would take care of her son.

She passed away that night. Next morning the villagers helped us to bury her. We had to hurry back home to our village as my mum was concerned about my sister and my brother, seeing that we had left them alone for a night.

When we got home, we took Sokha to register with our family. He was my mother's nephew and an orphan. The difficult thing about

Sokha was that he was a chatty child, he talked too much and was often stubborn and problematic. He did not want to stay with us for long. Once, he was supposed to come to Kork Romcheck labour camp with me but stayed with another woman. He kept telling everyone that our family was rich, that we had everything, cars, houses, etc. He put us in danger but luckily, nobody took any notice of what he said.

Then, he was struck down with malaria and died. Another family member wiped out. My mother lost her last nephew and it seemed that all the effort we made turned to dust.

16

I was selected to work with a group of teenagers. Our duty was to go into the forest to cut down and collect any small trees that we could find for use at the dyke site. Once the men had cut the trees down, I collected two or three of them along with other teenagers and carried them out of the jungle on our shoulders.

There were many wild mushrooms in the forest. Everyone picked them, along with any edible leaves that we could cook with the mushrooms. Some of the group hunted lizards, wild animals, birds, and anything they could find along the way while they were working.

It was fortunate that I could stay at home with my family after work. I enjoyed going into the forest every day as it gave me time to think and the Khmer Rouge soldiers were not present to guard us. Some of the boys would sing quietly or hum songs that they remembered from before the Khmer Rouge took power. When caught being involved in any anti-Angkar activities, you would definitely get a beating, but in the forest we were safe. I did not know what was in everyone's mind at the time, we did not talk or ask about where they were from or what our lives had been like before 1975. It was as if previous times no longer existed.

After a while, I was selected to join a group of ten men and move to an adjacent camp. They needed workers because so many young teenagers had died due to illness, punishment, and executions. Some died because they could not cope with the extreme heat or were exhausted with work and lack of food. No one dared to complain or refuse to work and those who did were condemned as leeches. At every meeting, the Khmer Rouge would tell us, "To keep you is no benefit, to destroy you is no loss."

The new camp was grim. There were many long rows of sheds built from bamboo with thatched roofs. There were no decks high off the ground to sleep on, so I found some straw, laid it on the ground, and used a rice sack as a mat. It was like animals sleeping in a barn. Some people were lucky to have a hammock and could sleep comfortably off the ground.

The next morning, I was given a hoe, two baskets and a pole made of bamboo. Breakfast consisted of a small bowl of watery rice with a pinch of salt. Hundreds of people worked in the same field building an enormous dike on higher ground. We had to carry soil from the low ground and bring it to higher ground. Each group of workers was given a target at the start of the day. Some dug the soil, while others carried the soil to fill the top of the dyke, but all of us worked from dawn to dusk. None of us knew the time, we simply worked until we were told to stop.

I was given both jobs, digging the soil as well as carrying it to fill the top of the dyke. My target was to dig out the soil from a hole of one-meter wide, one-meter deep and two meters long. The ground was hard, the hoe was weak, both my hands were blistered, and blood ran between my fingers.

That day, I could not complete the target. When everyone left the site to go back to the camp, I was there still digging with a few others. We were not allowed to leave the plot until the target was achieved. Darkness fell. I hoped that they might allow me to go but this was wishful thinking against the unforgiving Khmer Rouge. The soldiers made campfires, dotting them around us so that we could continue to work through the dark. The sky was clear, there was no wind and we were watched by the soldiers.

Soon, I could not go on any longer and as I finished filling a basket, I fell asleep on the ground with my head on the basket and the hoe laid down next to me. I could not remember how long I slept but I was awoken by a strong kick to my back. The soldier who kicked me awake pointed his rifle at me and shouted at me to get up and continue. I got up and carried on working. I did not have anything to eat that evening. I was eventually beaten because I still could not meet the target.

Quite often, maybe once a week, we were called to attend a concert or entertainment piece. Petrol-powered lamps illuminated a stage on which Khmer Rouge players performed. They were in groups of men and women, all in black uniforms, as was the regimented status quo. The girls had short-cropped hair and wore red scarves. All the men wore black pyjamas and carried guns or sickles depending on their role on stage. They were singing and dancing in the Chinese style and used loudspeakers.

It was awful but we had no choice but to sit there to watch. Some of us fell asleep but if the guards saw anyone close their eyes, they would wade into the audience with kicks and punches to wake up the offender, and anyone else in their way. The actors sang about the greatness of the Communist Party and how proud they were of their victory, exulting in the destruction that they had wreaked on capitalism and the Americans. It seemed to me that those of us from Phnom Penh city were their worst enemy.

Our camp area was situated a few hundred meters away from the area of the guards that was illuminated by white neon lights. We could see the lights shining in the distance. The Khmer Rouge enjoyed their life, rich in food and laughter.

Down in the camp, we did not make conversation with others, we did not make friends, and we were not interested in each other as any knowledge of others could put us in danger. To engage would be to care and when so many perished so often it was not wise to worry about anyone other than yourself. Hope never left me, but gradually what I hoped for became narrower and narrower. By now, all I wanted to be was survival for me and my family.

Nothing else seemed possible.

17

There was a man named Poun, who oversaw the camp and one day he ordered us to go to a meeting. He was tall, dark, with an evil face, and he had the power to execute anyone he wanted. Comrade Poun slept all day, had plenty of food, carried a gun, and wore the evil black uniform. Most importantly, he had a pair of proper rubber shoes, high-status watch, and sometimes carried a small radio on his shoulder.

All the men from my group, including the two brothers who slept by me, went to the meeting as instructed. The brother's had fair skin, which the Khmer Rouge did not like. As usual, we were told to sit in lines of tens. All of us were interrogated, questioned, and kicked if we did not answer the question to the satisfaction of Comrade Poun.

He asked me my name, my family background, and what my parent's jobs were. I answered his questions carefully, but obviously not as Poun wanted me to, and he began to rain slaps down on my head. I told him my name but lied about my family background. Then he started to pat me down.

He searched my shirt top pockets and found a small pouch that contained a gold necklace, a Buddha, and a diamond ring. The ring belonged to my father. It was expensive with eight diamonds in it. My mum gave me the pouch loaded with valuable items just in case we were separated. That way, I would have some gold and diamonds to exchange for food.

He took the pouch out of my pocket. I could not refuse or stop him. He opened the pouch and found the gold necklace with the ring attached to it. It was a dark night except for the light coming from the moon and stars, plus the neon lights from distance. The diamond was shining, flickering in the light and I watched it as he put it in his shirt top pocket.

I asked him gently, "Please, brother! Don't take my Buddha. That Buddha is to help me, protect me from illness. Also, it is from my mother, I will be ill if I don't have Buddha with me."

He responded that I would have the pouch back the next morning. Then he continued to question and interrogated another person.

After the guards told us to disperse back to the camp, I followed Poun and begged him to return my pouch. He coldly told me to go back to the camp or he would beat me again. I did not believe his promise that he would return my items and I could not sleep that night having lost what my mother and father had given me.

Next morning at dawn, I woke up earlier than usual. I did not see the two brothers. Their spaces on the floor were empty, but their baskets, poles, and hoes were still lying there. Where were they? Had they returned from the meeting last night? I discovered later that many had disappeared that night. The Khmer Rouge hated those with lighter skin, like that of the two brothers, because it signalled that they had Vietnamese heritage. Their mother was in the same group as us at the village and had told us about her half-Vietnamese, half-Khmer family.

Anti-Vietnamese sentiments were fuelled by the Vietnam-American War and echoed through the Khmer Rouge's ideology. It was normal to target non-Khmer people: Chinese and Vietnamese minorities. Some have speculated that under Angkar, racial differences were even more heavily scrutinised than the class ones. They hated those with light skin more than they hated capitalists.

I did not have time to find out or think too much about them as I had things to do and tasks to complete. I picked up the hoe, baskets, and bamboo pole, and walked straight to the main camp. I knew where Poun slept – it had a Khmer Rouge flag posted in front of the ground and it was the place where all the meetings took place.

I put the tools outside Poun's place, opened the glass door and found him asleep on his bed. I woke him gently, asking, *"Brother, brother wake up, where is my Buddha? I need it back."* He opened his eyes slightly and snapped back at me that I should be at work. I was brave again and persisted, *"No! I have a bad headache; I am not working today."*

He did not respond, rolled over, and went back to sleep. I glanced around his bed and found the shirt that he had worn the night before hung on the wall next to his bed. I found the pouch in his pocket, took it, and strode straight out from his place back to work in the field.

At midday, we had our usual break and I went straight to the pond where my mum waited for me every day. She brought me sweet potatoes that day. The pond was about 100 or 200 meters from the dyke site and next to the pond was next to a well, and a massive banyan tree that gave merciful shade from the sun. I found my mum and sister sitting under the tree waiting for me. I went straight to her and discreetly handed the pouch back to her. I told her how evil Poun had been, that he had taken the pouch, and the risk I had taken to get it back. The mother of the two brothers was also there and she asked me if I had seen her sons. I was not able to give her hope with my reply.

18

Battambang province is well known for rice production, it was the main rice supplying province for the whole country. Before Pol Pot introduced Year Zero (discounting all years and history before 1975), there were never any shortages of rice. But, after the Khmer Rouge came to power, we starved.

Before Pol Pot, we used to feed pigs with rice and banana stalks, the leaves from sweet potato plants and water convolvulus, now we dreamed of feasting on such fare. People stole ropes that were made from ox or buffalo skin to eat and they caught any insects or reptiles that crawled in front of them. I looked at their malnourished bodies, their haggard skin, and distorted faces. Whenever I caught a glance at my face when I gazed into the pond water, I did not recognise the face that looked back at me.

I had not had a haircut or any new clothes for four years. We were ordered to dye all our clothes black. I was very fortunate that I had been taught sewing at primary school in Phnom Penh and I could repair clothes for others, including the head of the group, which made me a useful member of the community. Because of this, some days, I did not have to work in the field and could spend a day or two in the camp mending clothes.

During those days on my own, I could do some thinking. I was shy, quiet and my thoughts were of my family and the uncertainty of the future. Occasionally, I missed my school, my studies, and my friends, I thought to myself that I could have been at medical school by now (my greatest wish had been to become a qualified doctor). At that age, everyone should have normal feelings, feelings of love or wanting to be loved. I did not have any of that. I kept my face covered with my *kroma* scarf and repressed any interest to talk or make friends.

Much later, my mother told me that some of the highest-ranking men in the group asked her if I was a girl, disguised as a man. They even asked her if they could marry me.

Because I was different and shy, it made me stand out and it made them curious. I told her to tell them to give us a pot of cooked rice or a whole chicken to eat first in exchange for knowing who I really was.

They kept me working at the construction site at Trapeang Thmor. I did not take any notice of the time, the day, or the month. It seemed that there were no weekends, no New Year's Day, or any celebrations whatsoever. There was nothing except work. The only thing that I noticed was the change in weather and soon enough, the rainy season started. The work at the construction sites had to be done and finished as soon as possible. There were more groups joining the site all the time from other camps. Most of them came with oxen and buffalo with ploughs. It was close to the rice planting season, so they all came to prepare the ground.

I did not see Comrade Poun anymore. He must have been moved to another camp. From time to time, I noticed new Khmer Rouge soldiers arrive. They were from different regions, the east and northwest of the country. Those from the eastern region were known to be more aggressive and when the mood took them, they executed people in the camp, even those who came from their own region.

One day, I was sent to look after the buffalo and oxen. It was my duty to take them out in the morning to the field to graze. If any of the animals went missing it was our responsibility. But it was better than working in the hard-labour camp, digging under the sun, and working under the unforgiving watch of the guards.

I had fifty or sixty oxen to look after and tended the herd with Pich Phirun. He was twenty, charming, tall, funny, and good-looking. He told me that he had been a ballet dancer in Phnom Penh. We talked a lot about our life in Phnom Penh as we kept our herd moving to look for better fields and grass. Sometimes, when we were bored and tired when the guards were not around, we would sit under the shade of a tree. Phirun would cover his face with his scarf, he would sing and dance, and I would laugh and laugh and forget about my worries for a while. Phirun was a talented man. He showed me how to make a hat from palm leaves which were very useful, and an item that everyone needed. On noticing our hats, the Mekorng (the heads of the group) ordered us to stay in the camp to produce hats for them.

Other men who tended the herds would spend their time hunting for crabs, frogs, or even snakes. They searched around the edge of any small pool of water to find them. If it were the dry season, they would hunt for wild rats in the rice fields, or under the hay, or in holes. They were easy to find if you knew where to look.

We had been tending the herd for about a month then we were called for a meeting where Phirun and I were selected to join the group of ploughmen. Equipped with a pair of oxen and a plough, we were sent to the fields. The head of our group was named Pup who had been our supervisor for many months, ever since we were working at the dyke construction site. Pup was short, muscular, and powerful, and was from the countryside, so he was used to living in the fields. At the meeting, we were given new clothes, a pair of black pyjamas.

I knew that I could not be a ploughman. I knew that it would break me. When we came back to the camp that evening, I told Phirun that I was going back to my family to the village that night. I did not know what got into my head at that time. Running from Angkar was forbidden. If I were caught, I would have been executed, but I could not bear the thought of being a ploughman.

Phirun listened to me quietly, and said, "If you are running away from this place, I will run with you too."

"No, you can't do that," I replied. "I am doing this for myself, you don't want to get caught. They will kill both of us."

He persisted, "No, I am definitely not staying here, I am going with you."

He made me promise to wake him up when I left.

That evening, I packed my few belongings without anyone noticing.

Around 3 am, I could hear the cocks crowing in the distance. I got up, grabbed my belongings, and left quietly.

Phirun was sleeping about half a meter away from me. I did not wake him. It was dark but with the light from the moon, I could walk without too much trouble on the uneven ground. I silently left the camp and walked through the fields, along the ridgeway in the rice fields, heading in the direction of my family's village. Soon, I could see the outline of the village.

I had been walking for a while. Suddenly, I could see the shadow of a person who came up at the side of me. It was Phirun.

He shouted at me, "Why didn't you wake me up? How could you leave without me?"

I did not have time to explain and just had to keep moving. We looked into the sky; we could see the morning starting to materialise.

The sun only fully rose when we reached our family home. Everyone except my mother was asleep and we told her that we had run away from the camp. We did not know what we were going to do now that we were back in the village. Suddenly Pup, the head of the group, turned up on his bicycle. I began to panic.

He came towards us and calmly asked, "Why did you two comrades run away from Angkar?"

We fumbled for an answer and eventually told him that we could not do the job that Angkar appointed to us. Then he said, "Why didn't you talk to me or tell me. You must return back to the camp immediately, now."

I said, "No, brother Pup, I am not going to the camp with you. You will execute me or punish me. I am not that stupid to go back with you."

Phirun had a small axe hidden behind the back of his waist. He told me afterwards that if Pup had physically forced us to go back with him, he would have used his axe. Pup still demanded that we rethink.

My mother remained silent.

Pup paused and then said to us, "Right, as you both refused to go back with me you must return the black uniform that Angkar gave you recently."

I said, "Yes, brother Pup, you have it back. I am happy to return it."

Phirun protested, "No, Neang (this was my nickname used in the Killing Fields rather than Sokphal) cut all buttons off the shirt. Angkar gave us that black shirt without any buttons, I wanted the buttons back."

Then Phirun took his short axe out, cut all the buttons and handed them to Comrade Pup. I was surprised how both of us dared to do that, we could have been kicked, beaten, or shot. Comrade Pup had a gun with him.

We were very fortunate that he did not harm us. I think perhaps he felt sorry for us or maybe he liked us as I used to patch his clothes for him and had looked after him when he was ill. Phirun used to make him palm hats and we both were nice to him. Or maybe we were just lucky. Once Comrade Pup had our uniforms, he did not bother us anymore and headed off back to the camp on his bike.

As soon as he left, we decided to split from each other. I decided to go to Kork Romcheck hard-labour camp. Phirun decided to go back to his village to his family. There was no time to lose.

19

I left my mum in a hurry without eating any food. My worry was that the Khmer Rouge might send other soldiers to arrest me and Phirun. I knew the way back to Kork Romcheck well, it was only about ten or fifteen kilometres from the village. The camp itself was on higher ground, around forty or fifty meters squared in the middle of a vast open field. There were no trees, or bushes to escape to when the heat ravaged us.

I arrived at Kork Romchek in the late afternoon, I was tired and unsure about how I would be received. None of the Khmer Rouge soldiers were around at the time, everyone was working in the fields, and I slipped inside the camp unnoticed. When the workers and guards came back, they could not be bothered to ask me any questions. I used to work there before, they assigned me my tasks, assuming I had been out to work somewhere else for a while.

That evening, I did not have anything to eat except the dry food my mother had given me. It was getting dark, there were black clouds in the sky, and the wind was picking up and the rain was coming. I had to find a shelter, somewhere to sleep. I had no choice but to lay my mat on the ground in a long row of stables where they kept oxen and buffalo. Despite my partial shelter, I still got soaking wet and was exposed to the cold and mosquitos biting me all through the night. My head was right next to a buffalo's feet, I could hear them moving and defecating, sometimes their faeces landed just next to my head with a horrible smell.

The next morning, I went to the canteen and stood in the queue for food. Then, I met the head of the group who allowed me to stay in his group. They put me in a group and assigned me a hut with three other boys of a similar age. Amongst them was Phally.

A boy named Vanna had a good job looking after the canteen. He was a cook and I never saw him collect water or chop any logs, which made him act in a bit of a big-headed way towards the rest of us. If he liked someone, he would give that person the better-cooked rice from the pot. He was friendly with Phally who was in my group. I remembered a man who oversaw the kitchen with Vanna. He wore a watch which was a symbol of status. If you dared to wear a watch, it meant that you must be an important person within the Khmer Rouge. The man did not do any hard labour, he just slept, got up, ate plenty of food, and looked healthy. Neither Vanna nor his friend from the kitchen ever went down to work in the fields with us.

Phally had a small part helping in the kitchen. He and two others carried food supplies, like cooked rice, soup, and water, to people working in the fields once a day. We all were pleased when we saw them arrive at midday with the food, balanced on their shoulders in the baskets. We could stop at midday to eat our food allowance: a small bowl of rice with a ladle of vegetable soup. What they called vegetable soup, however, was without vegetables – it was just water with bits of plants floating in it, tasteless. While we were working either in the rice paddy or in the dried ground, people always kept their eyes open for anything they could catch like grasshoppers, crickets, rice, rats, and snakes. I continued my technique of chewing raw grain rice while I harvested it. It destroyed my teeth but helped to keep starvation at bay.

Rice paddy in hard labour 1975 (Credit of DC – CAM)

I found myself in a different world, not the world that I used to live in. It was a world without compassion, love, or care for anyone. Some children were told to call their parents 'comrades', they were Angkar's children. There was no belief in anything except the Khmer Rouge.

I did not care to know anyone. Except for my mother, brother, and sister, I was alone. They were the only people that I cared about. While I was working at Kork Romcheck, I saved rice grain from my allowance and dried fish that I exchanged with other people to give to my mother. Sometimes, the guards gave us rice grain to cook ourselves instead of distributing it at the community canteen. Some used the rice to mix with plants, insects, rats, snakes, and fish that they had scavenged from the fields. I did not have the energy to go fishing or find rats in the field.

I took the food to my mother when I had permission to visit my family or on the rare occasion that I managed to pretend that I was ill or sneak out of the camp without anyone seeing me. I missed my family greatly, and I would go off to the village and return on the same day, just to see them.

One day, I had permission to visit my family, so I collected as much rice, salt, and dried fish as I could. The early morning was heavy with rain and the roads and fields were flooded. I could not swim, the water was up to my neck, and I was on my toes in the water. At that moment, I saw a dead body floating next to me. It looked so white and horribly swollen. I was terrified and, in my panic, I tried to move away as fast as I could, so much that I nearly drowned. The way to my village was completely cut off by the flooding so I made my way to someone's house where I had to stay overnight. I was soaking wet, they let me sleep at their veranda outside their house, where I watched the dark rain and cold consume the night. I was hungry and cold but more than anything, I was upset that I could not see my mum.

I was forced to return to the camp the next morning, exhausted and hungry.

From the beginning of the rainy season till the dry season when the rice was ready to harvest, the Khmer Rouge experimented planting different crops. They planted rice in the dry season too and tried to use the water left over from the rainy season to help the rice grow.

I was sent to work in the rice paddy, collecting rice seedlings, transplanting rice in the fields. Then I was tasked with looking after the rice fields by walking along with a hoe, checking if any broken dykes were to be mended. I had to keep checking the water level in each of the rice fields. I used to ride on a large waterwheel, called a *noria*. It was made from bamboo with paddles for two people to ride. We were watched constantly by the Khmer Rouge guards, AK47s slung over their shoulders, they would circle us, making sure that we did not allow the waterwheel to stop.

When it was time to harvest the rice in November and December, we were set targets each day and we stayed in the field until the target was met. Every day when we returned, we had to carry the harvested rice back to the camp. Then at night, after food, everyone had to go to work at the rice threshing yard until midnight. I was so tired, sometimes I fell asleep in the pile of hay. We were constantly watched and each morning a guard would walk from hut to hut to check if anyone had remained when we were supposed to be out working. Anyone who had stayed in the hut was called out, sat on the ground and interrogated. They were denied their rice ration if they did not work. Few could survive like that for long.

Strangely, in all the despair and labour, there were marriages at Kork Romchek labour camp. This was not a rare occurrence and, in my time, there, I witnessed as many as thirty or forty weddings. The brides wore black shirts, black wraparound skirts and a red scarf, and the grooms wore black pyjamas and a red scarf too. All their clothes were provided by Angkar. But they were nothing like our traditional Khmer weddings with all the colour and guests and joy. There was no happiness at camp weddings. Some of the marriages were forced, if any of the men wanted a woman, he could request Angkar to marry her and it was impossible to refuse Angkar. There were no wedding receptions or parties afterwards. In that time hardly any babies were born and if they were, most of them died quickly.

20

One day, we had to attend a meeting. I sat in front of a line of Khmer Rouge soldiers and although they were not carrying any guns, they looked important. The meeting was attended by men from different groups. We were told to gather our belongings and to leave Kork Romchek immediately. After we received our morning food allowance, we started to walk from the camp with fifteen others to Phnom Srok village.

Hot, red gravel along the main road soon blistered my feet. About midday, we arrived at Phnom Srok and were permitted to stop for a rest under a large tree in front of an empty brick house. When we sat on the ground in a circle, they called us to get our food allowance again. It was a surprise to receive a bowl of solid cooked rice and some dried fish. As good as the food tasted, it felt as if every mouthful were a trick. Were they treating us well before they would execute us? Was this the last dinner of condemned men? But nothing happened and after the meal we continued our journey on foot.

There were two ox carts with our group that carried food supplies and tools for work. We walked behind the carts in silence, through the forest and across the fields. It was nearly sunset when we were told to stop and set up camp for the night. Tired and hungry, we went to find wood and water to cook. We were on the move again in the early morning.

When we reached our destination, we set up camp and I was given a hammock – such a great comfort! I tied it up between the trees, high off the ground, safe from any crawling insects or snakes.

The next day, we had a meeting where we were informed about our duties, designating as a specialised group that would travel around repairing the essential dykes. Our duty was to check along the dyke for any subsided land that had been damaged by rain. I was selected to be a cook and to take care of the kitchen equipped with an assistant who fetched water and wood for me. I cooked rice and prepared food for our group of fifteen people. We had plenty of food supplies and every week we went to collect dried fish, beef, and palm sugar from the main food stock in Tonle Sap lake. Two men had to go with an ox cart and returned two days later with the food. We still shared cooked rice but there was always plenty to eat.

I felt lucky because this work was so different from the hard-labour camp while having more food than ever before. The camp was not far from my mother's village and Angkar allowed me to visit her. I saved some dried fish, rice, and beef for her, leaving early morning and coming back the same day to complete my work in the kitchen. I was happy to be there for a few months with plenty of food and the relief of not having to work in the labour camp.

At the same time in the village, I heard and saw new Khmer Rouge soldiers coming from the east. It was clear that our commanding soldiers were afraid of them. The eastern troops were known for their ruthlessness and for having no mercy. The easterners even accused the western Khmer Rouge comrades of being disloyal to Angkar. The cracks in the cohesion of the regime's supporters were starting to show and Pol Pot's people began to destroy themselves. Many of the Khmer Rouge troops and villagers began to be executed more and more ruthlessly. It seemed that they came to kill any civilian who had pale skin representing Vietnamese or Chinese heritage. Some unfortunate civilians in the village had been executed in broad daylight because of their skin colour.

One of my mother's friends, who was a teacher from Phnom Penh, was taken for execution along with her two young children. They executed them one by one by hitting their neck with a hoe so that they fell into a pit – the bodies stacked on top of one another. Somehow, my mother's friend survived the execution. When they hit her head, she fell into the pit, unconscious. When she woke up in the middle of the night, she found herself under a pile of dead bodies, with her two children dead. She climbed and crawled out of the death pit to escape and found my mother, to tell her of the travesty.

21

Three Khmer Rouge guards were listening to their songs and music and the news on their radio as we worked. The broadcasts proclaimed Pol Pot's victory against the Americans, fascism, and slavery.

A few months later, the three guards that supervised us did not seem as happy as usual. They heard on the radio that Vietnamese troops had invaded Cambodia and, as days passed it was clear that the while the Vietnamese advanced, the Khmer Rouge were retreating. Soon after, the three camp leaders disappeared.

I was sent to go to another place, along with a few boys. I am not sure how I got there but I can remember the image of an expanse of rice fields. There was no village, no houses at all but in the middle of the field was a hill with a few mango trees and a large pond full of lotus. Next to the clear, cold lake, there was a kind of open shed and a row of long shelters that were made from bamboo with a thatched roof. Next to it, there were piles of bricks and broken ovens and we deducted that it had been a brick factory.

We reached the hill in the late afternoon and were joined by about 25 other people of a similar age to us. They had been selected from a different group in a different area. Four of Pol Pot's soldiers were sitting, cool and relaxed, as they watched over us. We were unsure about what to make of them with their radios, watches, and clean black uniforms with sandals made from car tires. Why were they here and what they were going to do to us?

We were told to sit in a group of ten. I found a group but again they selected me to cook and two others to collect wood and water. There was some water left in the fields in small puddles of mud and sometimes we went out to find fish or crabs for food. I oversaw the cooking and mending any torn clothes for everyone while the head of my group made sure that I stayed in the camp to do my job.

Angkar told us that we were to train to be Khmer Rouge soldiers. We were designated a rifle each – I picked the lightest one that I could find, an American M16. They showed us how to clean it, dismantle and reassemble it. They gave us two magazines each full of extra bullets; there was no way to refuse.

All the boys were excited about it and had grand delusions of being great soldiers, so much so that they forgot who they were and where they came from. I remember one of them in particular. He was tall, dark-skinned, and no one knew his real name, but he was known as A Klork (Gourd). He was given the nickname Gourd because he was slow and timid but was harmless.

Every morning from six o'clock, I was sent with the group to train in the rice fields. We had to practice crawling on our elbows and aiming and shooting the guns at our imaginary enemy. At night, we took turns to do sentry duty.

I thought about my mum and family in the village. I could not contact them anymore, and I was scared that I would never see them again. Every day or night, I would pray to my grandmother, my father, and Kosal to protect me.

Punlork who was the same age as me, tall and fit as he was from a farming family became the head of the group. We were very friendly with each other, and he seemed to know about me. When we were away from people or on our night shift, we would talk openly about our past and our background. One night, we were lying on a pile of bricks looking into the sky. It was a clear night with many stars and Ponlork began to ask me about my family and myself. I told him the truth about how I missed my education and my home in Phnom Penh. In turn, Ponlork told me that he was educated, and his family was living in a village nearby. He said that he would take me to meet his father in the village one day. We spent so much time together which led people to make fun of us. A few times at night during our sentry duty, we were caught in heavy rain, strong winds, and thunder and lightning soaking us to the core. I considered our friendship as we huddled close to keep warm.

I made Ponlork promise that if we were sent to the battlefield, he would use the bullets that I had as I did not want to shoot or kill anyone. Ponlork understood, he accepted and promised me to do as I asked. Our friendship was reciprocated; we were both young, lonely, and away from our families, so we felt comforted to have found a trusted friend.

One day, we were sent to find extra cooking pots in the nearby villages. Ponlork and I left the camp in the morning and walked through till midday. We stopped to have a bath at a large lotus pond we found on the way. I was afraid of the sucking leeches, so I just wet my headscarf and washed my face. The only time that I could see myself was in the reflection of the water. We kept walking until we reached a quiet village. The village was green with more trees than people. Though the houses were now empty, Ponlork recognised it as his home village called Kamping Pouy. He still knew the village very well and we walked straight to his wooden house. It was a big wooden house high off the ground, supported by cement pillars. We climbed the stairs and found Ponlork's father in the house and the two of them talked for a short while.

Another morning, we heard gunshots in the distance, and we were ordered to grab our weapons and were rushed to the battlefield. We were not sure at the time who the enemy was and had to assume that it was the Vietnamese. Although the battlefield was not far from the campsite, there did not seem to be any Khmer Rouge soldiers in the proximity – we were on our own. Ponlork crawling next to me, we both kept our heads low to the ground. Bullets flew over my head, next to my ears but I could not see who was firing at me. I prayed to my grandmother, angels, and any spirit in the world to protect me from the bullets and I handed over my own bullets to Ponlork to use. I pretended to aim my gun and shoot in the air in front of me.

A few hours later it went quiet and the bullets stopped coming and we were ordered to retreat to the camp. Everyone was smiling and felt that we had won the battle. I did not feel anything except relief to return to the camp. When we all arrived at the camp, we were ordered to sit in line within the group. We were checked to see if anyone was missing or anyone injured. They checked our bullets to see if we used it and how many we had left. I gave all mine to Punlork and I showed them my empty magazines.

A day later around late afternoon, we were sent into battle again. Not far away we heard rifles, rockets, and the heavy sounds of engines on the ground. I presumed that was that of a tank. It was different from the first time; Punlork was not with me and I could not see anyone around me and all I felt was the shaking of the ground.

I could not remember how long we were on the battlefield. The sound of the gunfight came closer to us and soon we could hear Vietnamese voices in front of us. It was getting dark and I decided to leave the battle and leave the group to find a way to my mum. I did not see any Khmer Rouge soldiers around us at all so there was no one to stop me escaping back to my family. When the others in our group saw me leaving, they decided to follow. I was not sure of the way or where to go but I had to get away from the battlefield and the Vietnamese troops. The first thing in my head was to get rid of my gun. I found a dried, shallow pond covered with long grass. I threw the gun into the pond without any hesitation. Everyone did the same as me and we started to walk through the dark night. I did not know how many people were following me, but together, we cut a path through the bamboo bushes.

22

We walked until dawn and in the growing light I could see a few faces who had followed me from the battlefield. At sunrise, still wearing our black Khmer Rouge uniforms, we were out of the forest and into wide empty rice fields.

I led the group straight down the main road to my village, not thinking about the repercussions of wearing the black uniform. I just wanted to find my family as quickly as possible. As we approached the village, we stumbled upon something unfamiliar – three soldiers guarding a wooden barrier which turned out to be a Vietnamese checkpoint. When we approached, one of the soldiers asked me where we were going. I told him that I was going home to my mother in the village and they decided to let me walk on. I did not turn around or look back and continued heading towards my home. I felt safe, normal.

I was only ten metres past the barrier when I heard a Vietnamese soldier call out. When I turned around, I noticed that he had stopped Klork, who was pointing his finger at us from all the way back at the checkpoint. He had told the Vietnamese that he was with our group. The Vietnamese soldiers pointed their guns at us and ordered us to sit down on the ground. One of them gestured to Klork's right leg. He rolled back his black trouser leg up to just below his knees to reveal blood trickling from a wound on his shin. They wanted to know how he had come to be injured and asked Klork who we were and where we were going. Klork again pointed his finger at the rest of us, sat on the ground next to the soldiers, and told them that he came with us. The Vietnamese did not ask any more questions, but demanded that I come back, and then proceeded to tie us up.

They ordered us to put our arms behind our backs and tied them tightly. I begged the soldiers to release me and kept telling them that I was not part of the Khmer Rouge, that I was just here to see my mother. They did not believe me because we were wearing the black uniform, like Khmer Rouge fighters. The blood on Klork's leg did not help the situation or my pleas, it acted as evidence that we had served in combat against the Vietnamese.

I was furious with Klork for getting us into this predicament and probably angry with myself for leading us right up to the checkpoint without approaching more cautiously. I do not think that Klork had any family, he followed us because we were probably all that he had.

The Vietnamese used a single rope to tie us together in one line. We sat on the ground with the rope cutting into our tied wrists. Out of the uncertainty of the situation, no one spoke. Clearly, the guards were waiting for a superior to come and decide what to do with us.

When the superior arrived, along with an interpreter who could speak Khmer, it was decided that we were to be moved from the road and held prisoners inside a small structure which served as a brick oven. Being tied together made our movements clumsy and awkward. We sat as best as we could, our backs to the wall of the oven, trying to find a position that was the least uncomfortable.

The entrance to the brick oven area was closed, and we were plunged into darkness. I could not see anything, and I said to myself that that was it: we were going to be burned alive inside this oven.

I have no idea how long we were sat in the dark, but a glimmer of hope appeared when I heard the voices of my mother and my brother Sokbonn outside, begging the Vietnamese soldiers to release me.

I did not realise at the time, but someone saw what had happened and rushed to tell my mum in the village. She was crying and spoke to them in broken Vietnamese, telling them that I was not a member of the Khmer Rouge, but they refused to listen, and sent her away. We were in that oven for a day or so and then they moved us out. Despite the fear that still gnawed away at me, it was a relief to be out of the oven. I reasoned that if the Vietnamese were going to execute us, they would have done so already.

My hope stayed intact.

For the next few days, we remained as prisoners in Poy Char village. I was not allowed to speak to my mother, but it was a comfort to see her just a few metres away and hear Sokbonn's voice quietly crying and begging my captors to release me even if it was to no avail. Soon, we were transported in a canvas-topped truck to another village around fifty or sixty kilometres from Poy Char. Mother was there to see me off in the truck.

Many years later she told me more about what had happened when the Vietnamese first came to the village. With all hope gone of seeing her husband and returning to her home in Phnom Penh, and with her precious jewellery almost exhausted, the prospects of being able to barter for more food were bleak, and she had reached her limits. One day, she cooked a pot of rice and added fruits that contained strychnine and decided to end her life along with my brother's and sister's. She ate a spoonful first and the rest of the family followed. It was incredibly lucky that this attempt failed, and no one was seriously poisoned.

When the Vietnamese came and drove the Khmer Rouge out of the village, many families took the chance to leave, just in case Pol Pot's followers somehow returned.

Pich Phirun and his family were amongst those who left. As they pushed their cart past, he shouted to my mother to leave. If not, she might be forced back into the jungle with the Khmer Rouge. She told Phirun that she was waiting for me and my family hid in the village and waited, hoping that I would return.

It was a brave decision. If the Khmer Rouge would have returned to the village, they would certainly have taken my family back to the jungle or would simply have labelled them as traitors and would have executed them on the spot.

My mother and my family were lucky to survive the ordeal. They were not discovered in the village. Whilst she was in hiding, she found an old lady named Chantoo, who was Mr. Touch Phen's mother. The old lady had been abandoned by her family because she could not walk. My mother could not leave the old lady to die alone and she allowed the lady to hide in the old barn house with the rest of my family. My mum told me that she was lucky to pick up some cooked rice that the Vietnamese had discarded on the ground, washed it, and re-cooked it, so they had something to fill their stomach.

As a captive, I was sent to Kralanh district. My mother was able to use some of her last remaining gold to pay a man to take her by ox cart to where I was being held.

I arrived in Kralanh as a prisoner of the Vietnamese. They kept ten of us tied together in a barn near a river. In the morning, we were escorted to the river to wash and drink the water. We could not use our hands to scoop water from the river, so we had to lower our faces into the water to drink it. If any of us needed the toilet all of us had to go.

Twice a day they gave us a small bowl of rice each. One day while we were cleaning ourselves at the edge of the riverbank, we saw a man swim across to the other side. At that moment, the Vietnamese soldiers began shooting at the man, and we could see the splash of the water as the bullets chased the figure. The man disappeared beneath the surface; it was clear that escape was not an option and any attempt would be met with death.

Yet again, my mother managed to find me. She told me that all the family were with her and that they would follow me to the end. She forbade me from trying to escape, she had seen people accused of being members of the Khmer Rouge and then killed by the Vietnamese soldiers.

One morning, I was met with a terrible surprise. They took me to an abandoned barn. My arms, my wrists were tied behind my back. Hay was scattered in the middle of the barn, and wooden blocks were dispersed on the ground. There were two of them. One was a soldier dressed in full uniform and carrying a pistol on his waist. They ordered me to kneel on the ground.

The questions began.

They asked me about my name and family background. Whatever I answered, they never seemed satisfied. The soldier kicked me each time I delivered an answer that was not to his liking.

Eventually, my torturer decided that his objective had been achieved and the wooden block was placed back under my feet and the rope was released a little. I slumped to the ground. My wrists had deep, raw ravines circling them, and angry blisters marking the edges. I was returned to the group. No one seemed interested in asking me about what had happened. The silence expressed the fear that everyone felt. By now, my both wrists had swollen.

I still carry the scars from the torture by the Vietnamese on my wrists. Every time I see my scars, I am reminded of this time; it is something that I will never forget. My life was so unhappy considering that I had never done anything bad to anyone. Why did I deserve all this?

Soon we were moving again, this time to a prison in Siemreap province, about fifty kilometres away. Potholes pitted the road – a relic of the war and the Khmer Rouge's complete lack of interest in keeping the country afloat. It took half a day to travel a distance that would have taken an hour before 1975. The Vietnamese still maintained that I was a Khmer Rouge soldier which left me vulnerable to execution at any time.

A few days later, my mum and my family, plus the old lady who was abandoned, arrived at Kralanh District in a village called Kampong Thkov. They were staying in a temporary place with many families.

This temporary place was where my mother met Mr Nao Thuok, his wife, and his family. They would become very good friends. His wife was kind and she gave some food to the old lady. I met him again many years later. He is now working with the Cambodian government as Secretary of State.

He is like a brother to me.

23

Time vanished. Uncertainty prevailed since it was unsure whether the Vietnamese might send me further away or simply slaughter me.

One morning, we were forced to move without warning. This time we all were transferred to Siemreap in the northwest. Mother came to collect me that same day. All my family were in tears and told me that they would follow me. I was relieved to see that they all were together.

The journey to Siemreap was bumpy and difficult because of minefields. We arrived at the prison in the late afternoon. The prison had light-blue gates, high yellow walls, and was separated into two sections. There were vegetable plots in front of the prison, surrounded by barbed wire. All the female prisoners shared a large room and a wooden door led into the men's section.

As we set foot in the men's section, the stench of human waste immediately hit the back of my throat. The rooms were filled with prisoners of all ages. At the centre there was a deep well where male and female prisoners could wash together. There was no privacy.

I found a sleeping area in the only spot available. Mosquitoes picked their prizes, cockroaches scuttled, and rats scavenged. When it rained, the temperature dropped low during the night. I had nothing to keep me warm or dry, and whilst others slept with mosquito nets, I slept with just a piece of my *kroma* headscarf to cover myself. I was sleeping next to three old men in their fifties; they had also been accused of being anti-Vietnamese. They were nice to me, we got on well and soon became friends. I called them both 'father'. Father Tee, with a fair skin and a fat belly, was my favourite. They were from a village called Phnom Leap near Kralanh village. Fortunately, I got on well with everyone, even though I did not know their full background nor the reason for them being in prison.

Sister Pak Kdey was twenty-eight, had fair skin and was quite pretty. She was with another woman in her fifties whom I called mother Pha as a mark of respect. Both women spoke Vietnamese fluently and got on well with one of the Vietnamese officers, Thanh, who oversaw the prison. Thanh was handsome and powerful, with the ability to punish anyone that he did not like. Officer Thanh fancied sister Pak Kdey and would come to flirt with her whenever he could. Sister Pak Kdey used his interest to avoid doing the same hard work as everyone else in the prison.

Twice a day, each prisoner received a bowl of cooked rice and a ladle of vegetable soup. The soup tasted like boiled water without any flavour, but we ate it to survive.

Every day, all the male prisoners were sent to work outside the prison and were then called by the Vietnamese to line up outside the prison cell to get assignments. Some had to tend to the vegetable plots in front of the prison ground, whilst the unluckier ones were sent to cut wood in the forest. I was blessed that I was never chosen for that task. It was dangerous in the forest with mines littered everywhere. My job was to look after the vegetables and to "fertilise" the plants, for which the Vietnamese used water mixed with excrement from the prisoners. Only the maggots were content with food that the vegetable patch provided.

One day, while I was working on the vegetable plots, I suddenly heard my brother's voice calling me. I turned around to find my mother, Sokbonn and Bonnary sitting nearby under a tree. My sister and brother pretended that they were playing around my mum so as not to attract the attention of the Vietnamese prison guards. From then on, my mum sat under the tree every day when I was working on the vegetable plot. Having her near me gave me great support and hope. The stench of the human manure in the vegetable patch did not seem so bad after that.

Sometimes, she would steal a chance to wrap a piece of food in paper, make it heavier with a stone, and when the Vietnamese were not looking, throw it over the barbed wire fence. I would quickly grab it and eat it before I could get caught. Four months later, I was released along with sister Pak Kdey and ten other prisoners. I think that it was Officer Thanh's doing.

On the night that I was released, sister Pak Kdey came to see my mother and asked if she would allow me to go with her. Her plan was to escape to a refugee camp near the Thai border where she had family that would sponsor her to go to the U.S. Mother told me that it would be my decision, but I could not leave her or my family.

Sister Pak Kdey escaped to the refugee camp in Thailand the next day and Officer Thanh was left with a broken heart. I never saw or heard from her again.

Refugee camp

24

With no money and no hope of finding my father still alive, we decided not to return to Phnom Penh. We had fallen out of love with our home. Neither did Siemreap feel like our home.

Nothing is permanent in this life. During this horrific time, we lost everything. By the time we left the jungle we had nothing left.

We bumped into Uncle Carin, my mother's cousin, Aunt Neaov, and her three children. Although uncle Carin owned a bicycle repair business, he sadly offered us no help. Some people changed from bad to worse after Pol Pot.

My mother did everything to keep our family together and to scrape together a living. I remember her sitting under the hot sun, at the side of the road, together with everyone else trying to sell their goods, her *kroma* scarf over her head keeping her cool. It was quite a contrast with the past. In the old days in Phnom Penh, we used to run a very good business, with many people working for us. I had never seen my mum doing the selling on the road before, and it gave me great heartache.

Gradually, I began to find my feet again. I had found out that many people were travelling to the Thai border to import goods to sell in

Siemreap. The market was very busy with people from all areas buying imported goods and selling them in Phnom Penh and Vietnam.

With so many young men having been killed by the Khmer Rouge, some parents wanted me to be their son-in-law. A woman who had a stall selling breakfast on the side of the road asked my mother if I could go with her to smuggle cigarettes from Kralanh to sell in Siemreap. She had a daughter, was nice to me and called me son. I was a bit embarrassed but had to go with her and put my trust in her.

Before I could start my smuggling business, I had to sell two items I had left. These items were a light-green long-sleeved Montague shirt and a tailor-made pair of trousers from an expensive material. I sold both to a watch repairman in the market. He paid me a hundred grams of twenty-four karat gold, to be precise: five gold rings, in pieces. With that gold, I could begin smuggling goods with her. She knew a convoy driver, who allowed us to travel with him to Kralanh, hidden under the canvas roof to get us past the checkpoints on the road.

On my first trip, I took half of the gold and I bought twenty packets of cigarettes back to sell in Siemreap. I was worried that I would get caught at the checkpoints by Khmer or Vietnamese soldiers, but soon learned how to bribe. It was a success and I doubled my earnings. After that I went with the lady on a few trips and we bought and sold everything in twenty-four karat gold.

We were given a small piece of land just behind the market area, which was very convenient to do business and built a bamboo shelter there. During a day selling in the market, I saw the two men I had met in the prison on bicycles. They were also smuggling goods to sell in Siemreap. One of them and his wife, Sess, suggested to me that I should start smuggling with them. After assuring my mum that they would look after me, I decided to trust and join them.

Having been successful in several operations, I graduated to buying goods directly from Thai smugglers, close to the border. It involved longer, more dangerous, two-day journeys by bicycle.

I soon paid off the cost of the bicycle with all the profit I made. Everyone in our group enjoyed riding, laughing, and singing along the road together. It was memorable times with travelling companions, stopping at a pond for lunch or a little pause. None of us showed any weakness or worry, we just looked forward to our rewards when we reached the market. This way, I never felt tired of travelling by bicycle up and down the long journey under the hot heat from the sun. At 4 am every day I got up and started my journey to Svay Sisophon where all the smugglers exchanged goods with gold.

I felt that I had a lucky bicycle – it never caused me any problems on the road. Oddly enough, when it did break down, it seemed to be giving me a message, as often we would learn that we had narrowly missed robbers on the road. By breaking down and delaying my departure, we missed these potential dangers on the road many times.

My family was always on my mind since I was doing this to support them. I felt a heavy responsibility towards them, as we had nothing left and were desperate to survive. I would always remember my father saying before he left us that he trusted me to look after my mother, brothers, and little sister. It was my duty and responsibility to do everything I could.

We gradually began settling down in Siemreap. My mother volunteered to teach the Khmer language to children and to educate some of the women. In turn, she was elected to become president of the Cambodian women community in Siemreap. I was glad to see her happy.

My mother at her workplace with Mr Lor Pear and myself.

The smuggling business did well, and I made some good connections. Along the way, I learnt the Vietnamese language and made useful contacts with officers in the Vietnamese army.

Later, we became acquainted with a lady who was the wife of Mr Om Borey, a professor. Mrs Om Borey had a son who was the Police Chief in charge of Siemreap and was working under the Vietnamese.

I was offered the chance to catch a lift to Phnom Penh with a Vietnamese officer who was friends with Mrs Om Borey. I accepted and when we arrived in Phnom Penh, I went to see my old house that was occupied by other people. I went in and told the people who were living there that I was the owner of the property and I wanted to see if I could find anything from our past. They let me look around, but unfortunately nothing was left except a shell of the house that had been our home. The ceiling where our family silver was hidden had been hacked open and everything was gone.

I stood in the middle of my old house looking around at every corner and was flooded with painful memories. I left the house with a sense of emptiness and sadness. I loved my home but when I saw strangers living there and cooking on the marble floor, it felt alien.

The good memories had gone.

I told my mum the news about our house. In my heart, I did not want to be in Cambodia anymore. It did not have any meaning for me as I had been forced to move around from place to place for many years. I had lost all my close relatives and friends and had nothing to call home. Everything had been taken by the evil regime.

While we were in Siamreap, I used to travel to the Thai border with a convoy driver. He lived in Phnom Penh with his family and had a daughter who was two years younger than me. To my surprise, he and my mother arranged a wedding for his daughter and me. I was about twenty-four at the time and I did not want to get married at all. I was enjoying my single life and the business that I was cultivating.

In our hut, my mum told me that I was getting married. I had to agree and obey her even though I did not even know her and had even met the woman that was going to be my wife. Mother hoped that she could look after me and that we would have a family. We got married in a traditional Khmer ceremony in Phnom Penh with the few relatives we still had left.

Before the wedding, both parents agreed that my wife would be living with us in Siemreap. Soon though, my wife moved back to Phnom Penh to be with her family and friends. She could not live without running water and electricity, but we saw each other when I travelled to the capital city on business.

A few months into our marriage, she announced that she was pregnant. In the following weeks, I found that I was not myself. My mood darkened, I had headaches all the time and acted poorly towards my family. It was as if I were possessed.

During this dark period, I continued working. When I was checking my overnight bag for business travels before packing to make sure it was empty, I found a piece of handmade white string instead which dropped on the floor in front of me. I recognised it as the type made by a priest or a sorcerer which was said to offer protection from evil spirits. I studied the string and saw that it had a few pieces of flat grey lead wrapped around it. I knew for certain that nobody in the house had this kind of string. However, I was in a rush to catch the bus, so did not have time to investigate any further. I hung it by the front door and left for Phnom Penh.

I made it to the bus headed to Phnom Penh and sat on the roof next to a middle-aged woman alongside other passengers. Up top, the fresh air was cool, and it was not as crowded as it was below. I did not know the woman next to me nor did I want to talk or have any kind of conversation with her, but she kept looking at me as if she was interested in talking to me.

Despite my lack of interest in a conversation, she pressed me to talk. "You are not single. You are married to a woman who is not good to you." I smiled at her but did not respond. Although I did not believe her, it began to prickle my interest. Perhaps she sensed this and continued, "You are not well, having headaches continuously and you are no longer getting on well with your family. You are missing your mother, brother, and sister when you are away from them but as soon as you get home you feel as if you are fed up with them."

How on earth did she know this? But what she said next was the most shocking of all. "Your wife has cast some black magic on you." After I had spoken to her, I found out that she was a fortune teller and a possessed spirit.

When I got back home from my trip, my mum told me that she had discovered the string and had taken it to a monk and priest to find out what it was. They had told her that it was a very bad spell designed to split me up from my family. They advised her to destroy it straightaway.

A few months went by, during which my wife and I separated from each other while she was carrying our child. We never had an argument or fight and simply ignored the fact that we had a problem between us.

Then one day, my wife turned up with the baby in her arms. It was unexpected and I did not know what to say or how to react when I saw her with my daughter in her arms. "Are you coming back to stay with us in Siemreap?" She shook her head. Instead, she wanted me to beg and apologise to her parents if I wanted her to stay. I did not agree, why should I do that? I was not in the wrong, we had agreed to live in Siemreap and I wanted to stay with my family. I had just escaped the jungle and had no desire to go back.

I looked at my beautiful daughter, I felt sorry for all that had happened between us. They spent the night at my hut, and I took them on my motorbike to the boat to Phnom Penh the next morning.

We agreed to live separate lives.

My wedding in Cambodia

25

A few weeks later, a woman delivered a note to our door asking us to attend a meeting at a refugee camp. My mother hoped that the note was from my father and a wave of optimism washed over her. Against all odds, she hoped that he might still be alive and had finally found us. Together with the messenger I had to meet the writer of the note. When the time was right, I went to the refugee camp at the Thai border to check the situation. I arrived at the camp safely and met the man who sent the note to us.

I did not know how he found out about us living in Siemreap but it turned out that the note was not from my father, but from Phirunn, one of my mother's nephews. Together with his sister, he used to live in our house in Phnom Penh and my mum looked after them and provided food, accommodation, and work. I had grown up with them, even though they were much older than me. They were living on the Aid from UNBRO (The United Nations Border Relief Operation) in the camp. They were given rice and dried fish as an allowance and were supplied with bamboo to build their huts. There were many of my remaining relatives in the camp as well.

I did not know what to do when I met them, but in my mind was the possibility of also moving into the camp hoping that would change my life. Life in Siemreap was getting harder and there were many factors that I had to consider: I was getting older, I could no longer go back to education and I was stuck with my family and my mum to look after. Not to mention my marriage was on the rocks and my wife did not want to come to live with us. But there was another possibility, which was going to live in another country as refugees, if we were lucky.

When I got home, I told my mum about the situation and circumstances in the camp. Of course, she was disappointed to hear that the message had not come from my father.

Arrests and deportations to Hanoi were still occurring and soldiers continued to question us about our personal background. Furthermore, the Khmer Rouge soldiers were still launching attacks on some remote villages near Siemreap. So, we made the difficult decision to leave Siemreap and escape from Vietnam's communist regime.

Our house and family in Siemreap. The picture was taken just before we escaped to the refugee camp. It was a lovely home with my family in 1981. From left to right: Chan Bonnary (sister), sitting at the top Mrs Pan Penh You (my mother), Din Dina (orphan cousin), Chansokbonn Din (younger brother), myself.

26

It was an extremely dangerous journey to the Thai border. We negotiated a fee with a guide called Orn and set the date of our departure for October. In preparation, we told our neighbours that we were going to Phnom Penh for a few weeks. Leaving Cambodia, I felt nothing. The scars from the past were cut deep in my mind and I did not say goodbye to any of my friends. I was excited to leave and thought that if I could make it out of this country, I might have a chance of a different life and to fulfil my dreams. We locked the house and left it as it was.

It would be difficult to take our valuables. To lose them on the journey would be a disaster so we took precautions, melting down the rest of our gold into small flat rolls that we inserted into the collars, seams, and stitches of our clothes.

The first checkpoint that we came across was loaded with Vietnamese and Khmer soldiers, who ordered everyone to get off the bus and walk through the barrier. My sister, cousin, brother, and my mother walked past the barriers safely. I was not so lucky.

One of the Vietnamese soldiers took me inside their control office in private and searched me. As he was doing so, I could see out of the corner of my eyes that my little sister who had been carrying some gold hidden with her, played nonchalantly alongside the road picking up flowers off the ground. She then walked slowly past the barrier and waited at the other side. I prayed that I would be able to be that calm.

The checkpoint guard searched and touched me all over. He found the gold hidden inside the stitches of my top pocket, inside my collars, and the edge of my shirt. I was confused as to why I had been the only person on the bus to have been searched. Had someone tipped them off? I allowed him to take what he wanted without hesitation; to argue with them meant arrest. Then, he allowed me to get back on the bus and join the rest of the travellers.

When we arrived at Svay Sisophon it was the afternoon, and we hid inside a timber seller's house. Orn had told us to separate.

Although it was raining and the wind was growing stronger, Orn guided us out through the back of the house into the dark wood. It was a horribly dark night, and we became totally lost. My mother could not walk fast, since the ground was slippery and full of mud. Only the thought that we were edging towards a better life gave us the hope and energy to carry on.

Soon, we were deep inside the forest, far away from the road and I could not see any lights or houses nearby. Then, we reached a small river; we could not tell how deep the water was. Neither my mother nor I were able to swim, and we thought we were stuck at the riverbank. Fortunately, we found a large tree trunk floating in the water. All of us grabbed it and held onto it firmly, paddling through the water. I could not feel the riverbed with my feet but luckily, the river did not have a strong current, and we were able to float to the other side of the bank.

We climbed the bank and walked through the night behind Orn. The rain did not stop, and we were cold, soaking wet, and tired.

Orn told us that we were approaching our destination, but to us, it looked like we were in the middle of nowhere with only a wooden house in view. We were told to climb the steps and quickly get into the house. I instantly recognised my cousin Dina. She stood in front of the mirror checking herself out and combing her hair which exposed the diamond earrings that my mother gave her to wear on the road. She had ignored our orders to cover up her ears to hide the diamonds. She did not realise that flaunting the jewellery and giving out this information put us in danger of being robbed again. To make matters worse, she was such a blabbermouth, that she told people there that I had been robbed, but still had more gold and diamonds. This meant that we could not stay with them as our position had been completely exposed.

We had to take a break and stayed at one of the houses of Orn's relatives. But this relative told Orn what Dina had told her. She was not happy to hear this and decided not to stay any longer. We had to leave in the dark immediately.

And so, we continued our journey. All the children – my brother, sister, and cousin – went off with the guide before us. My mother and I were no longer following Orn because she had disappeared through the wood and bushes before us. Perhaps she thought that we could just follow her tracks.

The forest was completely flooded. There were many obstacles and dangers in such deep waters. I was mostly worried about snakes, but the floodwater also covered the footpath and hid the sharp wooden stems of plants. Nevertheless, we had to stay on the path – to venture off it could mean stepping on a landmine.

Dawn came. Others overtook us, taking the same path which gave us hope. We must have been on the right track to the camp. Some smugglers also overtook us, walking rapidly through the water. My mum was struggling, and her exhaustion meant that she could not walk much. Sometimes, she would slip and fall into the water. The water level varied, at times it was up to my knees or waist, making it difficult to advance.

During the entire day, we waded through the water until it began to get dark again. Mother could not go on anymore, the difficult walking and wading had left her worn out and tired. We saw fewer and fewer people walking past us now. Mother sat down and I joined her. We could not stop but she could not go on and told us to leave her there. The insects landed on us, resting.

Then a miracle happened.

Two men in their mid-twenties stopped and our eyes met, and I looked at them hopelessly. One of the men had a small axe wrapped in his scarf hung across his waist. He took it out and said, "Let's see what I can do, I think I have an idea." He then turned to my mother and said, "I can't let you stay here, it's dangerous." He used his axe to cut a small but strong tree. He tied their scarfs to make a hammock and tied it to the branch that they had cut. They told my mum to sit tight on their scarf and hold on to the tree trunk. They both carried her, the tree trunk posed on their shoulders. The men walked quickly while I followed behind.

It was getting dark, I had no idea how long we were walking, but they both seemed to know their way. We had no idea who these men were, but I did not have any doubts about them. They could have easily harmed or robbed us, but I believed my instinct that told me that they were both young, generous, and kind.

We walked and walked until we reached dry ground. The road soon became much smoother and no longer hurt our feet. In the distance, I could see some lights which looked like villages or houses. Neither of the men spoke, they both kept walking towards the lights. It turned out that we had arrived at the refugee camp.

I found out next morning that it was called Nang Chan camp and it was not the camp that we were supposed to go to Rythissen camp. There were many refugee camps situated on the Thai-Cambodian border.

That night, we stayed at one of the men's homes and he told us that he would take us to another camp the next day. I did not know their names, but I found out that they were soldiers in Nang Chan camp. Our host's wife was very nice, she cooked us rice and boiled eggs that night. I could not wait for daylight because I was so concerned about my sister, cousin, and brother, but I was exhausted after the night's events, so I slept.

I woke up to the sound of cocks crowing loudly. Now that it was daylight, we could not wait any longer and wanted to go to Rythissen camp straight away to meet the rest of the family. Both men took us on their bicycles. I did not know how I felt, I had nothing left; all our gold had been robbed by Khmer soldiers when we left Siemreap. These two men, however, were also soldiers but they were very kind and generous and had rescued us from the flooded forest. We would not know what would have happened to us if we were left in the forest that night.

I regret that I did not know their names or contact details. Only their strong kind faces are imprinted in my memory. If I found them again, I would pay my gratitude and tell them how appreciative I was, having helped us without asking for anything in return.

That day, I felt helpless. I could not carry my mother and was devastated when she told me to leave her. I could never have left her.

We arrived at Rythissen camp and joined my sister, brother, and cousin. The cousin we took in, like Dina, could not keep her mouth shut and had already told some people in the camp about the gold we were carrying. She told the family, which should have been fine, but they were still strangers to us.

Even though we lived in uncertain times, we were happy living in the camp. There was no guarantee that we would have an opportunity to go to another country so we contented ourselves with living in a small bamboo hut with a palm leaf roof, eating our meals together and waiting for our luck to change. I loved my freedom and felt proud that I could look after and support my family. Good friends visited me regularly, and our lives were filled with chatting and laughing.

At some time whilst living in the camp, we received news that our hut back in Siemreap had been attacked and destroyed by Khmer Rouge guerrillas. This confirmed that our choice to leave had been the right one. The remnants of Pol Pot forces often launched hit-and-run raids on villages, killing innocent people and destroying many houses. Being caught or taken as prisoners by them again would have been the end.

At the Rythissen camp, we were also met by my Uncle You Il's second wife, Aunt Sieak. She had six children, none of whom had died in the Killing Fields. She was in a relationship with another man whom she had met in the camp and they were having a baby together.

We could stay with her and helped her with her business. I had learned some business techniques. I learnt to speak and write Thai which was a huge advantage in doing business with Thai people.

Aunt Sieak knew that we had some gold, so she asked to borrow some from my mother, who agreed and sold a diamond ring that belonged to my father to lend the takings to Aunt Sieak. While we took refuge at her place, we all helped her with her business. She made fake medicine for Khmer smugglers to sell in Cambodia and to Vietnam, making a very good profit.

In the beginning, it was sweet and happy but then a few months later, our relationship with Aunt Sieak turned sour.

It became clear that my aunt's new husband had not had a good upbringing. He liked to drink and soon started acting nasty towards my mother. My aunt could not stop her husband because she adored him. But this change of events meant that we simply could not stay with them anymore, so we moved out immediately.

I started up my business as a middleman again, buying and selling to other Khmer and Thai people. The business went well as we had many regular customers. I enjoyed life and the freedom that the camp allowed.

In the Rythissen camp we had a Buddhist temple, Wat Prasat Serey, built in bamboo and occupied by many monks. The head of the monastery was a good monk and we visited the temple regularly bringing food to offer to the monks. My mother was very pleased that we had a Buddhist temple in the camp.

After a year in the camp, Prouch Borasy arrived. She was the daughter of Mr Prouch Vann, a relative of my biological father. Mr Prouch Vann had been a doctor, which was a death sentence under Pol Pot's regime, and had been executed. Prouch Borasy, or Peov as we liked to call her, was in her early twenties and my mother recognised her straight away. She was planning to escape to another camp called Khao-I-Dang which was a transit camp situated in Thailand. Anybody at that camp had the guarantee that they would get the opportunity to get to another country. Unfortunately, it was difficult to go to Khao-I-Dang because of tight security. Every camp had barbed wire around it and the Thai soldiers in black uniform permanently patrolled outside the barbed wire fences. No one dared to cross the fence.

Peov told my mum about her plan and that relatives were waiting for her in France. However, she had to get inside Khao-I-Dang camp first to get to France and had no money to be taken across the border. She visited us regularly, she knew about my business and many things which made my mum trust her and like her very much. Often, she would stay overnight with us in our hut and have dinner with us.

We had some trouble from the Vietnamese who would try to attack the camp from time to time. Everyone was on alert and prepared to run for their lives if that were to happen.

One night, Peov was staying with us as usual and was sleeping in the same area as my mum and sister. Our hut was separated with a thin wall made of palm leaves and bamboo and there were no proper bedrooms. At midnight, we woke up to the sounds of explosions in the distance and soon we were ready to take whatever we could to flee.

My mother did not keep any valuable gold and pieces of jewellery with her in case we were robbed and instead stored all our valuables hidden in the legs of a long bamboo stool. My mum panicked and asked Peov to help her to lift the stool to remove the valuables from inside the bamboo leg. Regrettably, she had exposed her secret hiding place to Peov.

After a rushed preparation, we realised that we did not have to flee, the night calmed, and we went back to sleep.

My mother went to temple on every special Buddhist day and on every special event. Sometimes, she even stayed at the temple till the afternoon, listening to the Dhamma talks given by the monks. At one special event at the temple, we all went in the early morning, bringing food and donations to offer to the monks. Prouch Borasy went with all of us on that day. I remember that in the middle of the ceremony in the monastery, Peov told my mother that she felt unwell and wanted to go home to rest, so mother told her to go and get better. We continued to stay until the ceremony had finished.

When we returned home later that day, we saw Peov was sleeping in my mother's room. As we walked into the house, we had an unusual feeling. Mother went to check her valuable items and was left in shock to find that all the gold and jewellery had gone, even the gold chain belonging to our regular supplier, Bann. Bann was Thai and Khmer from Surin in Thailand. When he was short of money, he borrowed some from us and would leave his twenty-four Karat gold chain to secure his loan.

Mother woke Peov up and asked her if she saw or had let anyone in the hut. Peov pretended that she had been asleep and said she was the only person in the hut, she had not heard anything else. My mum asked her and begged her again if she had mistakenly taken them. She denied it and swore on her mother's life that she did not steal those items. She declared that if she was lying, may her mother die. My mother was amazed that she compromised her own mother's life. However, only she knew where the hiding place was. We begged Peov to tell the truth and to return even half of it before we had to call the police. Peov still denied it and maintained her innocence, but the trust was broken, and we had no doubt that it was she who stole it.

My mother had no choice but to report it to the camp police. They came and arrested Peov. I could not believe what had just happened. Our relative had let us down and had betrayed our trust and care. We had a good day at the temple, only to later come home to this awful situation.

Then, we found out more about Peov. She had a lover, named Cheat who she had recently met in the camp and who was a charming, tall, and handsome man. Apparently, he had an older woman lover that Peov did not know about. Peov was secretly seeing him and had fallen in love. Both had planned to escape to Khao Ee dang together and they needed money to pay the guide. But she did not realise that he was using her.

First, she had relatives in France who told her to go to Khao-I-Dang as it was easier to get a sponsor in Khao-I-Dang. It was for this reason that Cheat was interested in her. Secondly, he knew that she was related to us and we had a good business and some savings. The police arrested him but released him afterwards. Peov was in the police cell for a few days and we went to visit her every day to see if she would confess.

On the third day of her time in prison, a policeman came and told us that Peov was in a critical state. She had black and blue rash marks over her face and body, and it was suspected that she had taken some poisonous substance in the cell. When we got there, she was unconscious, unable to speak and died later that day.

I thought, maybe it was a punishment for her bad actions. Was it because she had lied to us or had someone given her poison to cover this up? We never found the truth, or where our valuables went, or if she had even stolen it. Then we found that her lover Cheat had run away to Khao-I-Dang. We believed that she had passed all the gold and everything to him and sacrificed her life for him.

My mother was a strong-minded person, even when we had lost many things in our life. I saw her cry sometimes, but she used Buddhism philosophy to ease her pain and her past and we still lived in hope of a better future.

We have a special seasonal Buddhism ceremony that takes place only once a year, which the monks called Kathinak (cloth offering). Mother wanted to spend her money and contribute to the temple and we ended up spending more than 5,000 bahts on that occasion. I followed my mum's wishes even though we had lost a lot of money recently.

We felt content because we had fulfilled our wishes and hoped that our next life would be better.

Life in the bamboo hut was spent watching time go by, waiting for a miracle. Our future, we hoped, would be away from the camp. I had no contact left with anyone in Cambodia at all and whatever possessions we had there were never recovered.

We could not do anything apart from hope for a miracle.

* * *

A few years passed in Rythissen camp.

One day, I reconnected with Vanna (his real name was Phannaroth) who worked in the Kork Romcheck hard-labour camp, with me. I remembered him working in the kitchen and the night that he was tortured. He was training to become a medic in the American-run hospital. After a while, he started to visit us regularly and my mother became fond of him. He looked after her and gave her injections, put her on drips, and gave us some tablets he got from the hospital.

I never asked or spoke about what happened to him after he left Kork Romcheck or how he ended up in Rythissen camp. However, later, he turned out to not be a nice person. But for the time being, we trusted him, and he told me that Punlork, my good friend from the Killing Fields, was now living in Dangrek camp. He too was a medic and was training to be a doctor. To hear that, reminded me even more sharply of how I had been deprived of my future.

We also found a cousin who was my mother's niece and uncle You Ol's daughter, You Chan Sopha. You Chan Sopha left Cambodia before 1975, wanting an education in France. With the help and support of our mother, her parents were able to afford to send her to Europe, just a year before Pol Pot came.

We searched and found her through the Red Cross. Chan Sopha sent us a letter with some photos, money, and the promise to sponsor our emigration to Britain.

Now we waited for this miracle to come true.

Waiting for the miracle to come true.

With my sister Chan Bonnary Din in front our bamboo hut in Site 2.

27

Gunshots, grenades, and the rumble of tanks on the ground – the Vietnamese troops were attacking Rythissen camp. It was the past catching up with us. We fled our hut, grabbing the emergency items that we had prepared. I took whatever was in front of me: clothes, pots, pans, and as many bits and pieces as I could. I left our valuable unsold goods in the hut – we had to run for our lives.

I dragged my bicycle and put my little dog, Ninedy, on the back of the bike. My mother, sister, and brother followed me along with my mother's friend and Run, the nice old lady who used to be our nice neighbour in Phnom Penh. All of us ran for our lives in the direction of the Thai border. It was a horrible scene to see the old, the young, and mothers with babies running, terrified. We ran through long grass in the fields, not caring about any mines.

I was very tired, and I could not drag my bike quickly enough through the long grass fields. I was struggling to pull the bike with Ninedy sitting at the back. Run, who was moving quickly next to me, saw me struggling and told me to let him off the bike and he would follow us. Sadly, Ninedy turned around and ran back to the camp. I could do nothing to stop him as there were so many people and guns exploding all around us. The ground shook with the sound of heavy vehicles. We had no time to find Ninedy and so yet again I lost a dog. My sister, who was running next to me, was also very upset about our loss.

Eventually, we reached the Thai border where we could see the Thai army in their black uniforms. They were stopping, checking, and searching everyone to make sure that no Vietnamese soldiers were able to sneak into Thailand. We were able to stop a few hundred meters inside the Thai border, staying close to the monks for protection against robbers or any unscrupulous Thai soldiers who might want to prey on the vulnerable refugees. We heard that some girls had been raped and killed – life no longer seemed to have any value.

That night we slept in the bamboo forest on the ground around a bonfire to protect ourselves from snakes.

Every refugee in the bamboo forest waited for news. Since we could not return to the Cambodian side of the border, the United Nations created a new camp. Blue plastic sheets became our unstable and rickety roof.

After much deliberation, my mother decided to pay a man named Sarik, to smuggle her and my sister Bonnary to Bangkok, so that she could telephone her niece, Chan Sophia, who lived in England, about the situation. The journey to Bangkok was dangerous, not to mention illegal, but she decided to take the risk. The smugglers hid my mum and sister under canvas in the back of their pickup. At every checkpoint she was nervous, hearing them talk in the Thai language that she could not understand. Fortunately, they let them pass. Meanwhile, I was waiting in the camp for a few days with my brother and my cousin Din Dina.

We made camp quite close to the group of monks, especially the chief of the monastery, Venerable Pin Sem. He was kind and concerned about our safety and whenever I had any free time, I went to venerate him, listening to his advice and learning more about Buddhism. He encouraged me to become a monk as it was an opportunity to learn and keep myself safe from danger. From a young age, I always believed in Buddhism but never learnt or practised it seriously. I have seen sadness, sorrow, death, and many horrible things in my life, so I thought, maybe I should try to find peace as a monk. But would my mother be happy to see me become a monk? What would her reaction be? Many questions ran through my mind.

To be honest, I do not know why I decided to become a monk, but I agreed to be ordained as a novice in the bamboo forest by Venerable Pin Sem. I was told that the Lord Buddha ran away to become a monk when he was twenty-eight years old, an age similar to mine. I thought that maybe I would become a monk for a few days until my mother came back.

It was my destiny and I ended up being a monk for two years.

After the ordination ceremony, I was not allowed to go back to stay with my family and had to stay within the group of monks at the temporary temple. I stayed next to my teacher, and due to my knowledge of many languages, including Thai, I became Venerable Pim Sem's assistant.

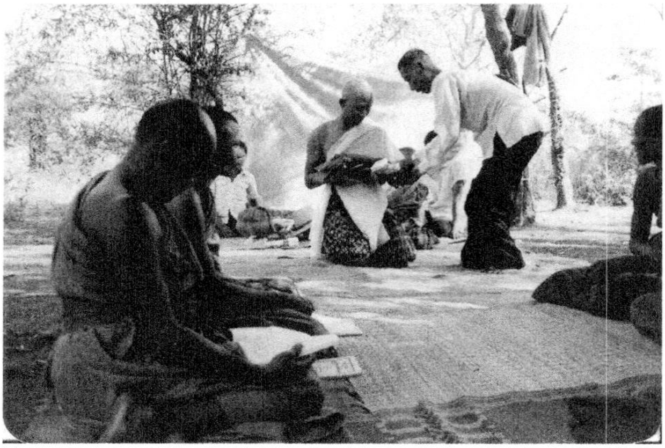

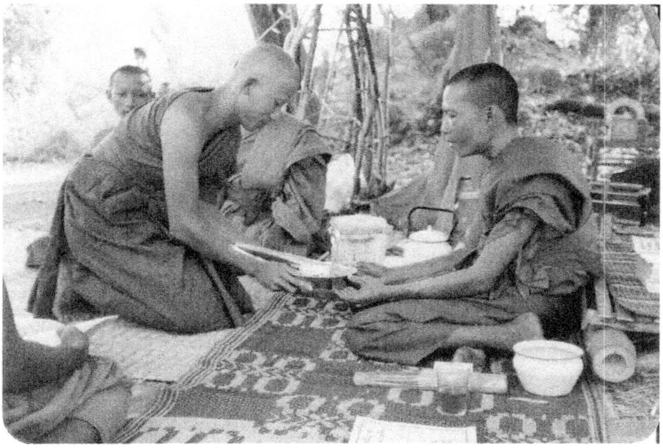

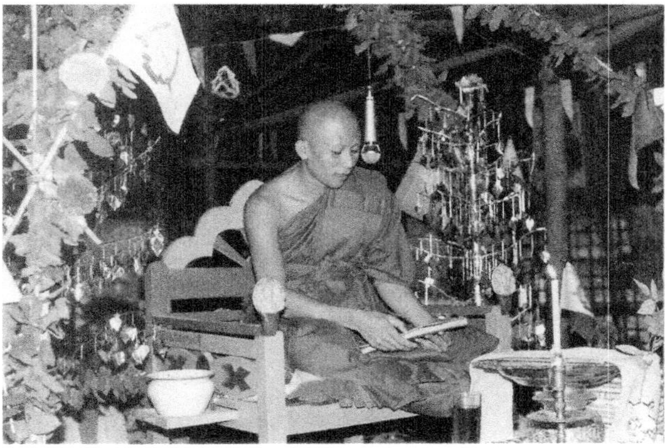

The next day, my mother returned from Bangkok. She had managed to speak to Chan Sopha and had informed her about the situation, but all that she could do was to tell us to be patient. My mum was pleased to see me settling down in a new lifestyle as a monk. I had been given the opportunity to learn about Buddhism. I could not compete with young monks as they knew Pali, the language used for chanting.

I had to get up at 4 am before sunrise to attend the group chanting in the shrine hall. Then we had breakfast together in the group offered by people from the kitchen. Everyone had to follow the rules. I followed the practice as a novice for a year, then as a venerable (*Bikkhu*) for another year.

We moved from the bamboo forest to Site Two camp and had to start over at a new place. This time, my mum chose to stay next to the temple, coming to visit me almost every day. Sometimes, she brought food to offer to the monks.

Punlork and his brother came to visit me at the temple.

I had the responsibility to look after the temple's donations and teach young novices. The monks received breakfast offered by the Lay people, the locals, at 7 am, after which I taught the young novices for an hour. After that, I had to go out with the group of monks equipped with my arm bowl (monk's bowl) to receive food offerings. We walked barefoot and stopped in front of people's huts to receive their offering and blessed them.

At Site Two camp, whilst I was a monk in the temple, Punlork appeared. He had been with me in the Khmer Rouge training camp in 1979. Now it was 1986. I did not ask him where he had been since then. He came to see me at the temple unexpectedly and I was pleased to see him looking well and to know that he was working in the hospital as a medic in the Dang Rek camp which was next to our camp. I now regret that I did not ask him about what happened after we ran away from the battlefield against the Vietnamese. It is funny that I still remember a simple little conversation that we exchanged. Punlork had asked me if I would allow him to touch my feet. I said, "No you can't!" I was a monk then and this was not deemed appropriate.

I was very pleased to see my long-lost friend, Punlork. Even though I wanted to, I could not hug him, or hold his hands as I was embarrassed, and it was an inappropriate action as a monk. I wish that I had allowed him to touch my feet. He was very pleased to see me, perhaps he was affectionate towards me. A few years ago, I heard the news that he passed away.

My mother, my sister, with Punlork standing next to me.

A layman named Soy did not like my position close to the head teacher Venerable Pin Sem. He began to spread rumours and defamed me, destroying my life as a monk.

He reported to my head teacher some untrue stories about my mother who continued to visit me. He was a troublemaker and I was unhappy to hear him criticise my mum, so I went to ask my head teacher if I could resign from being a monk. He declined my request and did not want me to resign.

But with this defamation and slander, I wanted a change. I discussed this with some monks and asked them if they could assist me with the ceremony. Three of the monks agreed to assist me so that I could prepare to disrobe and leave the temple.

I came home and left my life at the temple, but my head teacher was unhappy that I had left. Now, I had to adapt back to a normal life again with my family. I started training at the American hospital at the Site Two camp to become a medic.

A few months later, a miracle occurred.

I was working in the hospital at the office as usual and suddenly a white Red Cross car stopped in front of the office. A Thai man got out of the car and walked into the office asking for me. He told me to go home and start packing. We would be picked up in two hours. He did not say where, but I knew it was good news and a miracle would be on its way.

My mother told my cousin, Dina, to pack while we went to say goodbye to my head teacher at the temple. We left for maybe ten minutes, but when we returned home, we found that Dina was gone. We looked for her everywhere but could not find her. The Red Cross arrived, and we had to leave without her.

We were taken to Arannya, the transit camp in Thailand, where the refugees had medical checks. We were waiting for Dina for almost two months. It turned out that she had been hiding in our next-door neighbour's hut at the time we were looking for her. It was yet another disappointment for us.

Phal, the next-door woman, had two children and we always helped and gave her anything we could. How could Phal betray us by letting Dina hide in her hut and lie to us, we failed to understand. When the Red Cross interviewed Dina later, she told them a pack of lies. Supposedly, she had been treated badly by my mother. We thought that she was either resentful or not quite right in her head. Fortunately, the Red Cross interviewed some people who knew us, and who set the story straight. In fact, Dina had secretly fallen in love with a man in the camp. He brainwashed her, suggesting that if she stayed, there was a chance that the Red Cross would help them both join us. Unfortunately, it did not happen like they had hoped.

We passed the medical tests, were sent to Soun Plu, which was yet another transit place for immigrants and refugees in Bangkok situated close to the airport. After we passed all the medical tests required, we were ready to leave Soun Plu.

After twelve hours in the air, we landed in Heathrow on the 5th of August 1987 at 6 am. It was the start of a new chapter and a new life.

28

The day we arrived at my cousin's in Basingstoke, on the 5th of August 1987.

Things were still difficult. I will always be grateful to the relatives who took us in, but after the excitement of our welcome wore off, the relationships sadly turned sour. We had been given a double room that the four of us had to share. There was no bed, so we slept on the floor, but we did not complain – we were so grateful to be alive and safe.

Being very motivated and eager to get on with my life, I went back to school for a few months and quickly learned English. Soon, I had a job at a printing company, *The Basingstoke Press 75 Ltd*.

I worked hard to earn money for my family with £100 a week wages and got weekend work at another job, using this money to pay the rent and food at Chan Sopha's place. I exerted myself to try and show that I was a keen worker. I was trained to use the paper plate making machine and I worked seven days a week because of our need for money. I learned everything that I could, and the company was good to me. I got to be in the company promotion video for Xerox and in many company adverts. I started right from the work floor and gradually worked my way up to the top. I was a quick learner, self-learning, and a hard worker. I hardly ever had time off sick because I was concerned for my job and did not want to have a bad record in the company.

Soon, we found a three-bedroom house to rent. Our relatives were not happy that we were leaving and from the day we left, my mother's niece Chan Sopha froze us out. We had lower rent and we managed to save some money which enabled us to travel to see other relatives in France as soon as we received travel documents.

First, we visited my mother's sisters-in-law in Paris. When we arrived at the bus station in Paris, we met Aunt Chreng Darlin, my mother's sister-in-law. She told us that her husband, Mr Om Sophan was killed in battle against the Vietcong in 1973 and that all three of their children had died in the Killing Fields. The majority of Cambodian survivors never ask in detail what happened to others in the Killing Fields. Instead, they simply ask how many people of the family was left, who is alive and who is dead. Because we were kind-hearted and grateful for the chance to move to England, we decided to try helping others to have the same opportunity. It turned out to be a mistake.

We sponsored four people from the refugee camp Site Two but were sadly enough only used by them. One of them was a man who I met in the hard-labour camp, two other men and a girl from the Site Two camp. It was my mum's idea because she was so kind and trusted people. There was no benefit to me, but I obeyed my mother and her wishes in the same way I had agreed to marry a woman that I had never met.

After the people we sponsored were successful in England, they all turned into different people. They were disrespectful and rude to my mother.

Despite all of that, we never stopped being kind and trusting people. We thought they would do the same to us, but it was a very bad and painful experience.

29

1995 was the first time I returned to visit my home in Cambodia with my mother. Before the plane touched down in Phnom Penh airport, I looked through the small window to see the city from the air. It was hard to restrain my emotions. I cried and felt so sad and had such mixed feelings about going back. We left our home in Phnom Penh in 1975 with all our family and relatives. Now only two of us were returning.

We went to see our old house. As I saw it for the first time in seventeen years, I realised that I had no feelings for it anymore – it was no longer my house. The mango tree had grown bigger and higher and other people were living there. The house number and exterior were still the same, but the people who were living there, now ruined the house with extra and untidy features.

This country has done so much damage to my life. It is fortunate that I am alive to be a witness.

The next day, we went to visit Chanlok village where we had been forced to live with the villagers in April 1975 for a few months before we had to suffer in the jungle. Although the scenery had changed, the same people still lived there. We were pleased to see them, but again there were only two of us. No one could understand the sadness in our hearts.

I also saw Pich Phirun, who I had known in the labour camp at Trapeang Thmor, was had now become a famous and rich actor. Perhaps I should not have been surprised to find him different from the character that I knew in those terrible times.

We went to meet my former teacher, the monk, Venerable Pin Sem in Siemreap. He was pleased to see us after so many years. We had not seen one another since 1987. We saved up money for them and were able to hand out about 50 polo shirts to donate to the temple and orphan children living there. Boys and girls were told by the monk to line up in rows to receive these gifts. They were very pleased and excited. It brought tears to our eyes.

After our visit, Cambodia became a much wealthier country. And in 2017, I went back to Cambodia on holiday with Nick, a friend of mine. He was the one who had arranged the polo shirts for the orphans. I had been thinking of visiting the last place that we were in the Killing Fields: Poy Char village and the dyke construction in Trapeang Thmor. Aine, from Siemreap, was kind enough to take me there. It took us two hours to travel by car from Siemreap to Poy Char village and Trapeang Thmor dyke.

Along the way, I had many things on my mind, amongst them were many sad memories. I wished that my mum would have still been alive to accompany me, since she had always wanted to visit Poy Char village and Trapeang Thmor dyke. Deep down, I was upset and excited at the same time, and felt curious to find out what had become of it. I was wondering if the people we had known in the Killing Fields were still alive. The view was totally different from what I knew from back in the old days. The road led directly to the village and I saw Kork Romcheck, the hard-labour camp, on the way.

My memories came back with sadness and tears. I felt so fortunate that I was able to return to find the place and to see Aine, whose roof we had stayed under. Mrs Aine was still alive and well, and she remembered me. We met at the house where we used to live temporarily, still looking the same from 1976. We cried and talked about our past and memories.

I wished that my mum could have been there with me.

Whereas my mother had enjoyed visiting Cambodia, my own feelings gradually changed. My native country had merely become a place to visit relatives and see the country, it was no longer my home. My home, land and dreams were taken away from me a long time ago.

However, this was softened by a very special friend, His Excellency Secretary of State Mr Nao Thuok and his family. He afforded me his time and hospitality on my return trips changing my views towards the new Cambodia. I thank him very much for doing this.

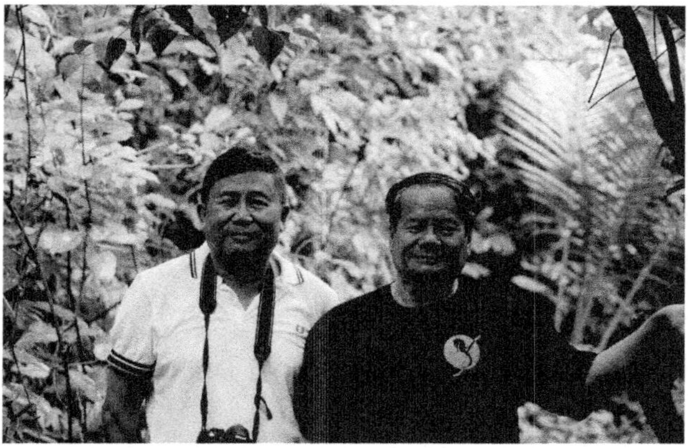

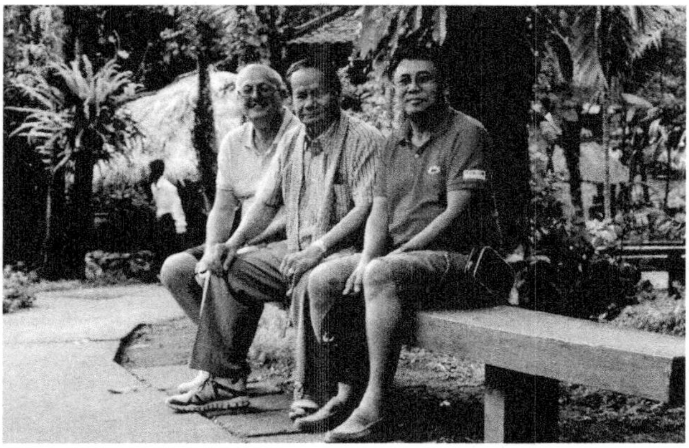

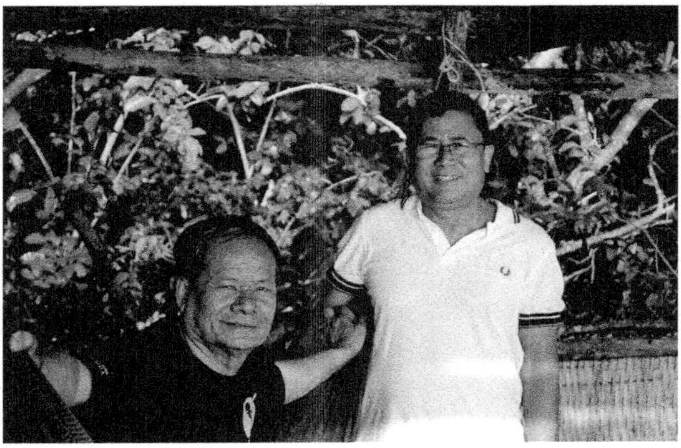

30

In the year 2000, my mum had a minor stroke and was admitted to Basingstoke general hospital. A few weeks later when she could move her left arm she returned home. She insisted on visiting Cambodia the following year later, so in 2001 we travelled together to Cambodia, along with a few other people, to fulfil her wishes.

Although she was fine and happy during our holidays, oddly enough she kept saying goodbye to her relatives and friends and was giving everyone lots of gifts. She even gave her own handbag – the one that she was using – to another relative. She told them that this would be her last trip to Cambodia. I kept saying to my mother that she was being pessimistic and that she would surely be visiting Cambodia again.

We came back to England and celebrated my birthday on the 27th of September with my mother and family. At the weekend, I went to stay with a friend in Gosport.

Whilst I was trying to put my shoes at the door, my mother told me that I had been a wonderful son. I felt overwhelmed by her words and kept quiet. I did not consider myself deserving of her words, I just felt that I did my duty and respected my mother – this was the Cambodian way.

On the 17th of October, I came back from work and had dinner with my mum as usual. The next morning, I thought about calling her to ask her for the ingredients of how to make a fish sauce for Khmer dishes. But then I thought that I would wait and ask her when I get home from work; it was the biggest mistake I had ever made in my life. I should have called her, then she would have answered the phone and would have talked to me for the last time. From then on, if I think that I should call or speak to someone, I pick up the phone straight away and call them.

Around lunchtime, I had a call from my sister to say that our mother was in a very bad state. I had suspected the worst and rushed home in tears. When I got back, I found my mother was sick in her bed, unable to respond or move. I quietly told her that I was there. She never regained consciousness and went into a coma that same day.

I stayed in the hospital by her bedside. I could not sleep; I was exhausted and could not drink or eat anything. On Friday, I was at my mother's side from morning till around 5.30 pm. The nurse, who probably noticed how tired I was, told me that I should go home and rest. Mother seemed stable at the time. If anything changed, the nurse would call us.

Since my house was just literally ten minutes away from the hospital and I was very tired, I agreed to leave my mother to have a short rest. My sister and brother were there, keeping her company. When I got home, I felt very upset, empty, and cried. I could not accept the fact that this was happening so soon. I sat in the sitting room in front of the Buddha statues, lit candles, and said my prayers. I prayed, "Mum if you have to leave us, you can leave now. I wish that you have a good journey to a better place in heaven where you can be with Lord Buddha. I love you very much, but I don't want you to suffer anymore."

I was just about to finish my prayer when suddenly the phone rang. It was my sister calling from the hospital, saying that I should come to the hospital quickly. Our mother's heart and pulse were both deteriorating. I ran to the car and raced to the hospital.

When I arrived, she slipped away peacefully as I held her hand. It is impossible for me to describe how I felt to see my mother leave us. It was sad to think that I was an orphan now. She was my very best and trusted friend. Even when we were going through terrible times in the Killing Fields and she brought me up with love and care.

I had seen many people die before my eyes. I saw my father for the last time when I was six, my grandmother, many relatives, and friends, but to see my mum on her last day had truly made me ill.

A few days later, I felt pain in my chest, like I had been punched by a powerful force. I presumed that is what we call a broken heart. I shaved my hair and wore black clothes for 90 days to pay my respects according to the Cambodian tradition. It took many years for my pain to ease.

Anytime I travel on an aeroplane, I look at the skies and wonder where my mother is. Is she cold or hungry perhaps?

In 2007, the Basingstoke Press 75 Ltd, that I had been working for from 1988, went into administration. The firm was taken over by a company called Synergy and I was made redundant in 2010. I was unemployed for nearly ten months, during which I suffered from depression, high blood pressure, and shingles. I felt very sad that I could not find a suitable job with my qualifications and experience in printing, but the internet had brought printing directly to people's homes. Therefore, I went to college to retrain and study again.

During my part time employment at Sainsbury's, I was invited to give educational talks about my experiences in many schools and many special places.

I was very fortunate that the Holocaust Memorial Day Trust and Aegis Trust invited me to share my life experiences. Also, I have been working as a freelance translator helping with the judiciaries, filmmakers, documentaries, and the BBC World Service. I have had the opportunity to do much charity work because of the support I have been given by Sainsbury's.

I really appreciate the chance to give talks to school children about the genocide in Cambodia and my life experiences. Hopefully, this will help school children become aware of the horrors of war and understand that this should never happen again.

In my heart, I believe that my mother would be proud of me.

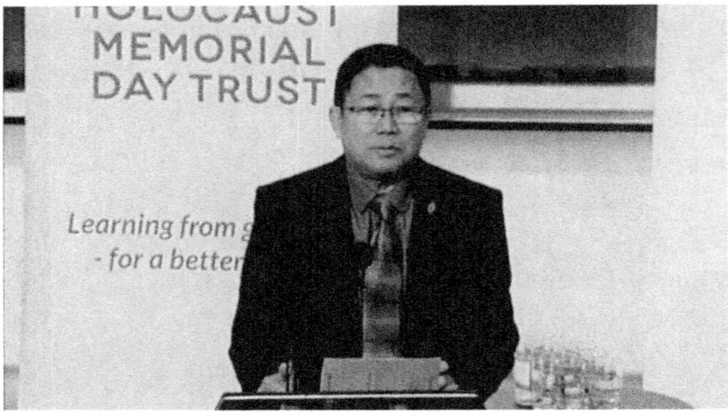
MEMORIAL
DAY TRUST
Learning from
- for a better

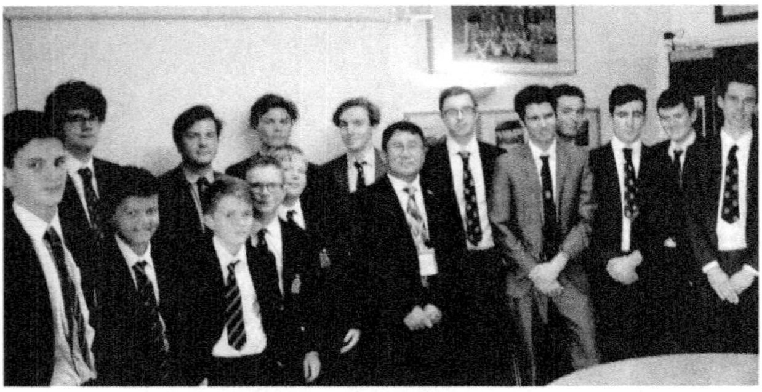

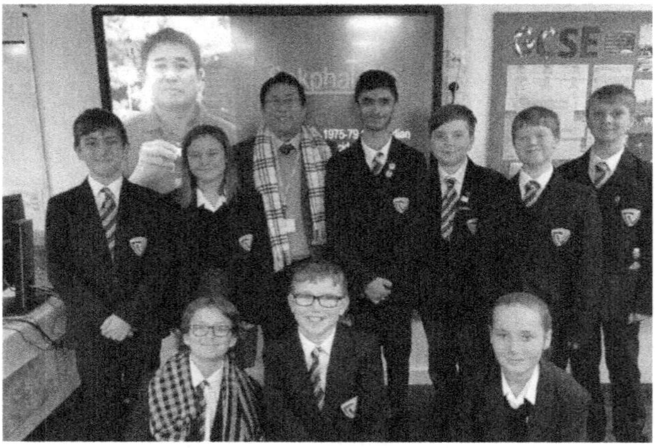

At Hampton School in London.

Addressing the public and honorary members of the Basingstoke Council including the Mayor on Holocaust Memorial Day, the 27th of January 2019.

On the BBC documentary about the Genocide in Cambodia (2019).

A special memorial reception at The Royal Palace with His Majesty Norodom Sihanouk the King father and Her Majesty Monineath Sihanouk, The Queen Mother of Cambodia. Same evening an invitation by His Majesty the King Norodom Sihamoni to join Cambodian ceremony festival called 'Water festival, Salute the Moon' at the Royal Place.

On the 9th of February 2017, I was fortunate enough to meet His Royal Highness Prince of Wales at St. James Palace, regarding the Holocaust Memorial Trust activities.

A meeting with Prime Minister David Cameron at no. 10 Downing Street in London, on the 27th of January 2016.

On the 27th of January 2020 with Prime Minister Boris Johnson, regarding my charitable work and The Holocaust Memorial Day Trust.

On the 22nd of May 2019, I was very fortunate to have an audience with Her Majesty the Queen of England. More surprisingly, in November 2019, The British Empire Medal for services to The Holocaust Memorial Trust and the Genocide was awarded to me.

I am very proud to have been able to share my life experiences, and the uncertain and dangerous journeys throughout my childhood till adulthood. Hopefully, my story would give some exhortation to future generations.

On the 19th of October 2018, I was invited to attend the conference with the Cambodian Prime Minister Samdech Decho Hunsen in Belgium and on 6th July 2019 in Switzerland.

On the 6th of July 2019 with H.E. Hun Maneth in Switzerland.

On the 18th of October 2018 with Samdech Krolahom Sar Kheng, the Cambodian Deputy Prime Minister in London.

Printed in Great Britain
by Amazon